D1478522

WITHDRAWN

The Linguistic Shaping of Thought:
A Study in the Impact of Language on Thinking in China and the West

The Linguistic Shaping of Thought:
A Study in the Impact of Language on Thinking in China and the West

ALFRED H. BLOOM
Departments of Psychology and Linguistics
Swarthmore College

LIBRARY
BRYAN COLLEGE
DAYTON, TENN. 37321

 LAWRENCE ERLBAUM ASSOCIATES, PUBLISHERS

1981   Hillsdale, New Jersey

84223

Copyright © 1981 by Lawrence Erlbaum Associates, Inc.
All rights reserved. No part of this book may be reproduced in any form, by photostat, microform, retrieval system, or any other means, without the prior written permission of the publisher.

Lawrence Erlbaum Associates, Inc., Publishers
365 Broadway
Hillsdale, New Jersey 07642

Library of Congress Cataloging in Publication Data

Bloom, Alfred H
    The linguistic shaping of thought.

    Bibliography: p.
    Includes index.
    1. Psycholinguistics. 2. Thought and thinking.
3. Chinese language--Psychological aspects. 4. English
language--Psychological aspects. I. Title.
BF455.B562   401'.9   80-27753
ISBN 0-89859-089-2

Printed in the United States of America

To my father

Contents

Preface

Fourteen years of interaction with the Chinese language and its speakers have alerted me to certain important differences between the Chinese mode of speaking and thinking and that of speakers of English. These discoveries are not only exciting in themselves. They increase sensitivity to what Chinese speakers mean. They heighten awareness of the biases implicit in the way English speakers speak and think; and they compel me to challenge the assumption, currently lurking within the field of psychology, that languages have little impact on the shaping of cognitive life.

The research reported in this book was supported by a grant awarded by the Joint Committee on Contemporary China of the Social Science Research Council and the American Council of Learned Societies for the year 1978, by a stipend from the National Endowment for the Humanities for the summer of 1975, and by research grants from Swarthmore College.

I would like to thank for their individual contributions: Margaret H. Bloom, Susan Blader, Susan Campbell; Chen Ta-tuan, Sydney and Mimi Chu, Pamela Crossley, Benjamin Elman, Joel and Arline Epstein, Lila R. Gleitman, Gu Wan-ch'ing, Heng Hsiung-jeng, Doris and Jimmy Ho, Ronnie Hsia, Herbert C. Kelman, Hugh Lacey, Cecilia Lee, Mei Guang, Mr. and Mrs. Pi, Michael Posner, Harris Savin, Vincent Siciliano, Benjmin K. T'sou, Urfie, Richard W. Wilson, an anonymous reviewer, my students at Swarthmore past and present, and the subjects who participated in the experimental research.

I would like to thank Winnie Vaules for her unfailing cheerfulness and for her consistently fine work.

And, in particular, I would like to thank Roger Brown for his continuing intellectual guidance and personal support.

The Linguistic Shaping of Thought:
A Study in the Impact of Language on Thinking in China and the West

Introduction

A NEW INFRASTRUCTURE FOR LANGUAGE AND THOUGHT

Does the fact that the Chinese lexicon carves up the semantic domain of the English word "reason" into a highly differentiated set of lexical concepts imply that the Chinese reason about reason and reasons in a more differentiated fashion than English speakers do? Does the fact that the Chinese lexicon includes words roughly equivalent to the English terms "suggestion," "mental perspective," and "meaning" but has no term directly equivalent to the English word "idea" imply that English speakers have an idea that Chinese speakers do not share? Does the fact that the Chinese language, unlike English, commonly uses distinct terms to distinguish "if-then" relationships from "if-and-only-if-then" relationships imply that Chinese students are, on that score at least, better fitted for first-year logic than their American counterparts? Does the fact that the English language, unlike Chinese, provides a distinct means for shifting from talk of people or acts being "sincere," to talk of "sincerity" as an abstracted property imply that English speakers are inclined to think about being sincere in a more detached way?

The question of whether the language we speak may shape the way we think rarely fails to excite the imagination of anyone who considers it for the first time and rarely fails to hold, from that point on, at least a lingering fascination and intuitive appeal. When bilingual speakers of two linguistically unrelated languages are asked whether they think they think differently when using each of their languages, they almost invariably answer "yes." When English speakers, who have extensive experience with monolingual speakers of non-Indo-European languages, are asked whether it is their impression that speakers of the non-Indo-European languages think differently from the way they themselves think, as a result of

1

language, they likewise just about invariably answer "yes." When translators of works drawn from literary traditions of unrelated languages are asked whether there is a language/thought barrier to overcome in translation, they usually find it hard to surpress a smile at so "naive" a question. Yet when psychologists are asked whether they think languages shape thought, they are as likely as not to say "no." When linguists are asked whether they think languages shape thought, they are as likely as not to respond that the question is not one with which the discipline of linguistics should concern itself; and when the work of the dominant empirical traditions of psychology, philosophy, and linguistics for the past fifty years is scanned for treatments of the question of whether or not languages shape thought, it quickly becomes evident that within these traditions that question, for one reason or another, never seemed to be a legitimate one or a relevant one to ask.

OVERREACTING TO WHORF

The surprising rejection by the empirical community of this rather compelling question stems partly from the fact that the work of its principal American proponent, Benjamin Whorf (1956),[1] quickly became associated with some rather untenable claims. Some read in Whorf the claim that the categories in which men and women speak not only influence but exclusively determine the categories in which they think. Yet these readers were well aware that children think about dolls, mothers, rattles, crawling, and even finding lost objects behind couches before they learn to speak and that adults make beds, drive cars, spice dishes, recognize faces and respond to complex emotional situations without recourse to words, and so rejected Whorf's ideas. Others read in Whorf not only the claim that the languages men and women speak exclusively determine the categories in which they think, but the still more deterministic claim that the first languages individuals learn determine those categories conclusively and immutably. This second group of readers were even quicker to reject Whorf's ideas for, in the first place, they shared our intuitive impression that we can learn other languages and in so doing master to a significant degree at least whatever new conceptual divisions of the world such learning requires. Secondly, they knew that speakers of every language borrow lexical concepts from other languages and invent new ones on their own and so cannot be prisoners for life of their primary linguistic worlds. And thirdly, they found Whorf's reasoning a self-contradiction for, according to their interpretation

---

[1] See also Sapir, 1921, and Humbolt, 1903–1918.

of his theory, Whorf, as a native speaker of English, could never be sufficiently free of the categorical hold of the English language on his thoughts to understand, no less explain, the conceptual structures of the Hopis or Shawnees—the very structures upon which he built his theory of the relationship of language to thought. Finally, still other readers reacted to Whorf on more purely methodological grounds, reading into his work the claim that any observable difference in lexical or syntactic categorization across two languages must entail corresponding differences in the way the respective cultures see the world. They rejected his ideas for they well knew that accepting such a claim would lead them quickly to absurd conclusions—to the conclusion that, for instance, because English has one word "bank" meaning both river bank and financial institution while French has distinct lexical terms for each of those meanings, English speakers must think less differentiately about the two kinds of banks than their French counterparts; or to the conclusion that because English uses "will" to mark the future, whereas French has a distinct set of tense markers, English speakers must have a less distinct and more volitional concept of future time than the French; or, finally, to the conclusion that because the English expression "Everyone loves his wife" means both "Everyone loves his own wife" and "Everyone loves some particular other person's wife," English speakers must confuse those two interpretations in thought.

In fact, Whorf never seems to deal squarely with the question of exactly to what degree a first language or any language determines the shape of thought—hence, the diversity of interpretations of his work. But it is clear that the reactions against Whorf's ideas were somewhat extreme. Rather than reformulate the question "Do linguistic categories exclusively determine thought?" into "When and in what ways do linguistic categories shape thought?" and reformulate the question "Do categorical differences across languages necessarily entail corresponding cognitive differences?" into "Which linguistic differences entail corresponding cognitive differences?," the critical reactions to Whorf effectively branded his work and, by implication, any further inquiry into the links between language and thought, as too riddled with conceptual and methodological imprecision to be taken seriously.[2]

OPPOSING ASSUMPTIVE FRAMEWORKS

But critical reactions to Whorf's work alone are not sufficient to explain why the enticing question he posed has been persistently slighted by the em-

---

[2]For discussion of Whorf's ideas and reactions to them, see Brown (1958); Cole and Scribner (1974); Crick (1976); Hoijer (1954); Laitin (1977); Romney and D'Andrade (1964).

pirical community. What seems rather to constitute the principal explanation is that to consider seriously the idea as Whorf saw it of a relationship between language and thought, for the past fifty years psychologists, philosophers, and linguists would have had to violate one or more of the principal substantive and/or methodological tenets of their respective disciplines.

Behaviorist Psychology

The fundamental assumption of the Behaviorist school of American psychology is that there is no such thing as thought. There is only behavior. The things humans say, the operations they perform, the reactions they have, the acts in which they engage in any given situation constitute nothing more than an integration of the responses (and generalizations from those responses) that they have been reinforced to make to the various components of the given situation or to similar components of similar situations from which they can generalize. Since there is no thought, the Behaviorist cannot legitimately ask whether and/or how language might affect thought. He can ask perhaps only whether and/or how reinforced linguistic behaviors might generalize to play a role in and thus affect the outcome of other kinds of behaviors, such as the manipulation of mathematical figures, the decision to buy a house, the way a lecture is organized, etc. But within the assumptive framework of Behaviorism there is no reason to suppose that any one subset of learned behaviors should generalize to affect any other given subset of behaviors in any special way. Hence for the Behaviorist, not only is there no such thing as thought, but there is no reason to suppose that those learned behaviors the layman might count as reflections of his linguistic abilities should bear any special relationship to those behaviors he might count as reflections of his cognitive abilities. In a Behaviorist world, in other words, there is no basis or motivation for entertaining seriously the possibility of a relationship between language and thought.

The Philosophy of Language Tradition

In his famous article, "On Sense and Reference" (1892), Gottlob Frege compares language to a telescope pointed towards the moon. The moon is likened to a referent, an entity within the non-linguistic world to which language, the telescope, points. Sense, the perspective provided by language on the external object, is likened to the image of the moon projected on the inside mirror of the telescope. As we shift the sense of our expression from "the celestial body closest to the earth'' to ''the first celestial body upon which man has landed'' to ''the only natural satellite of the earth,'' the linguistic perspective we gain on the moon changes, but the thing (i.e., the moon) to which we refer remains constant. Analogously, as we shift the telescope from one viewing point to another, the image of the moon projected on the internal mirror of the telescope changes, though the moon itself remains invariant. The eye of the observer at the lower end of the telescope views the moon via its reflection in the internal mirror. The impression the eye receives from the reflection of the moon is likened to subjective thought or idea. Frege's magnificent image lays the groundwork for serious consideration of the question of whether and how language affects thought. Language, with its own senses or meanings, its own perspectives on the external world, constitutes the telescope. Thought lies below the eyepiece. The question to be investigated is how language, the telescope, through the sense perspectives it offers, affects thought—how the images reflected in the internal mirror of the telescope influence and/or determine the perspectives through which the subjective eye views the world. But, rather than proceed with such an investigation, Frege leaves aside consideration of the relationship between the telescope, its internal images and the observer, and concentrates instead on clarifying relationships between the telescope, its internal images and the external world, on clarifying the ways through which linguistic expressions via their senses relate to the things and/or states in the external world to which they refer. In such sentences as ''X believed that Y is the case'' and ''Z fancied that Y is the case,'' for example, the expressions ''X believed'' and ''Z fancied'' are shown to relate directly to the external world, while the expression ''That Y is the case'' is shown to refer to a sense, a linguistic perspective on reality, rather than to the world directly.

Part of Frege's motivation for concentrating his attention on the upper end of the telescope (i.e., the relationship of language to the world) at the expense of the lower end (i.e., the relationship of language to thought) stems from his adamant stand against ''psychologism'' deemed irredeemably intuitivistic. Part seems to stem as well from an implicit assumption, shared also by Frege's successors, that the sense categories of language, the perspectives language offers us on the world, are equivalent to the significant categories of thought. To clarify the links between linguistic expressions, the senses they carry, and the external world is then equivalent to clarifying not only the ways we speak but also the ways we think about that world. And thus, the lower end of the telescope can safely be ignored without risk to the success of the philosophical enterprise. Whatever his motivation, however, the very fact that Frege turned away from the lower end of the telescope to concentrate his attentions exclusively on the upper end, had the effect of initiating a 75 year long philosophical tradition of continued exclusive concentration on that upper end.

Bertrand Russell (1905), for example, extends Frege's analysis of the paths through which linguistic expressions, via their senses or, for him, "logical forms," relate to the external world. He observed, for instance, that although at first glance one might suppose that the word "unicorns" in the statement "Unicorns do not exist" refers directly to the mythical exemplars of one-horned beasts, such could not be the case, for to refer to something, is to presuppose it exists; and, thus, if the word "unicorn" refers to unicorns, it must presuppose that they exist. But the statement says that unicorns do not exist. Hence, if "unicorns" refers to unicorns, the statement as a whole must be self-contradictory. But it does not seem to be. So, Russell argues, the word "unicorns" must not act as a referential term. He proposes the alternative interpretation that what we are in effect saying when we say "Unicorns do not exist" is that there is no (X) such that (X) is (i.e., fits the description of) a unicorn, with X the only component of the sentence that refers or potentially refers to anything in the external world. This translation into "logical form" lays bare the links between the linguistic expression itself and the external world and as such clarifies the conditions in the external world necessary to evaluate the truth or falsity of the statement. The relationship of our language to the world to which it refers becomes clearer, but not its relationship to thought.

The Logical Positivists[3] move forward in the same general direction, with their goal defined in an even more demanding way—not only to lay bare the links between linguistic expressions and the external world, but to demonstrate how each sentence of English can be translated by mediation of its "logical form" into a sense datum language—a language composed uniquely of natural categories of sense experience.

Quine (1960) severely undermines the Logical Positivist position when he argues that for at least the overwhelming majority, if not for all the words and sentences of natural languages, translation into anything resembling sense datum terms is quite impossible. Imagine defining a "bachelor" or a "theory" or a "counterfactual" in visual, auditory, and/or tactile terms alone, or validating the sentences, "That's a bachelor," "That's a theory" or "That's a counterfactual" on the basis only of visual, auditory, and/or tactile cues. There is, Quine contends, in the first place, no way to divide sense data, independently of language, into discrete units in terms of which the referent of a word or sentence can be represented. Secondly, with the possible exception of the most concrete words of the lexicon and the most concrete sentences of the language, words and sentences do not stake out their referential domains on their own, but do so only via a host of mediating words and/or sentences—if not the entire interconnected net-

---

[3]See Ayer, 1936, among others.

work of our verbal world. We know to whom the sentence "The bachelor just bought a new car" refers not by virtue of our knowledge of the perceptual characteristics of bachelors, but by virtue of other more abstract information we know about bachelors in general and other information (i.e., other words and sentences) we know about the individual being singled out. It is impossible then to lay bare for each word or sentence individually the links that tie it to the external world—impossible, in other words, to accomplish what the Logical Positivists had been trying to do. But Quine's demonstration that their quest and, by implication, the quest of the tradition of which they were part, was ill-conceived, did not have the effect of shifting his or its focus of inquiry to the lower end of Frege's telescope, to the question of the relationship between language and thought.

Drawing on his commitment to Behaviorism, Quine describes our knowledge of language as consisting merely in an array of words and sentences linked to each other and to perceptual stimuli via reinforced associative bonds. He likens this network of verbal elements and reinforced links to a giant arch, with the most concrete words and sentences of the language comprising the feet of the arch, anchored by reinforced associational links to objects, properties and events of the perceptual world, and with the most abstract words and sentences of the language lying at upper levels of the arch, supported by reinforced interverbal associations to each other and to the more concrete words and sentences lying below. We might learn, for example, the words "red" and "orange" by being reinforced to use them in relation to red and orange things, the word "color" by being reinforced in turn to use it in relation to the words "red" and "orange," and then the word "spectrum" by being reinforced to use it in a specific relation to the word "color." The language arch we thus build, moreover, functions not only as the basis for our language use but also—which is the same thing for Quine—as the structure through which we make sense out of the constantly and infinitely varying world of sense experience, through which we impose organization on that world. Our knowledge of when to respond with the word "color" is equivalent to what we would generally call our understanding of the concept color. The links we have been reinforced to make between the word "electron" and other words and sentences in our semantic web constitute the totality of our knowledge of what an electron is.

Quine's arch is again a magnificent image. It effectively dramatizes the internal interconnectedness of our linguistic world, its indirect relation to the world to which it refers and its infinite capacity for creating increasingly complex and abstract perspectives on that sense data world. But at the same time his image leaves undifferentiated the internal structure of the linguistic world that it describes; and it is again built on the assumption, borrowed in different forms from both Behaviorism and the philosophical tradition, that language and thought can be treated as one without affecting the outcome of the scientific enterprise.

Wittgenstein's Challenge to Whorf

By contrast to both the Fregean tradition and Quine, Wittgenstein does confront the question of whether there might be a thing called thought that is separate from and thus susceptible to the influence of language. Ironically, however, his conclusions in the *Philosophical Investigations* (1953) serve only to thrust the question still further from the center of scientific inquiry. In that work, Wittgenstein argues that a language consists in nothing more than a complex array of meaningless verbal tools which are manipulated by language-users, like the pieces in a game of chess, to achieve desired effects. Some manipulations are designed to elicit emotional reactions, others to elicit a behavioral response, others to impart information and still others to direct the listener's attention to a particular object or to induce him to consider a novel idea. The meaning of an individual word or sentence is its use, the effect it is designed to achieve. Moreover, as the context in which an individual word is used changes, so does its effect and so, therefore, does it meaning. Compare, for instance, the use of the word "thought" in "The thought crossed my mind," "His thoughts on the matter are worth considering," "He is deep in thought," "The thought of that dragon scared me" and "I thought you wanted me to write a shorter poem." Thus individual words and sentences cannot be said to have consistent or discrete meanings, nor can they be said to refer via such meanings in any consistent way to objects in the external world.

It is our failure to recognize this fact about language, Wittgenstein contends, that has led us to mistakenly assume that we can make use of language as a tool for furthering our understanding of the mental world. We mistakenly assume that because we have words such as "thought," or "reading," or "understanding," there must exist structures or processes corresponding to them; and it is these presumed structures and processes which we then rely upon for orienting our investigations of the mental world. But if "thought," "reading," and "understanding," as well as any seemingly more precise scientific terms we happen to coin, merely constitute a set of meaningless verbal tools, lacking in any consistent application, which we manipulate in multiple and highly variable ways in talking about the mental world—in playing that aspect of our language game—then we certainly cannot reliably make use of them as analytic tools for investigating that world. This is not to imply that, according to Wittgenstein, there is no mental world, no level of cognition separate from language, nor that language might not exert an important influence on that world, but only that we cannot make use of the words our language provides as keys to an understanding of that world. Unfortunately, however, we have no other means at our disposal; and, thus, any understanding of the mental world and, therefore, its relationship to language lies beyond the limits which the very nature of language places on our cognitive capacities. For Wittgenstein, then, the question of whether or not languages shape thought makes sense to ask, but it is impossible to answer.

The Structuralist School of American Linguistics

Given its own guiding assumptions, the Structuralist School of American linguistics, could no more grant serious consideration to the question of the relationship of language to thought than could its psychological and philosophical counterparts. In the first place, Bloomfield (1933), the founder of the school, accepted from the Behaviorists both the assumption that there is no such thing as mental structure upon which language might leave its imprint and the assumption that language reduces to a set of learned behaviors with no particularly interesting relationship to that set of behaviors one might label cognitive. And the link he forged between American linguistics and Behaviorism continued to pervade, at times implicitly, and at times explicitly, the development of his field. But even more fundamentally responsible for the reluctance of the structural linguistic tradition to consider seriously the question of whether languages shape thought, was the fact that tradition stood and stands principally committed to exclude from its realm of investigation any question of the relationship of language to anything else, in favor of concentrating exclusively on developing empirically accurate, maximally generalized and parsimonious descriptions of language structure. Only by consciously limiting its focus of inquiry in this way, practicioners of this tradition believe, can linguistics both maintain its status as a rigorous empirical science and achieve its primary descriptive goals.[4]

Thus it is not difficult to understand why the idea that languages might shape thought as an empirical question fell into disrepute. Not only had Whorf's work elicited rather too negative reactions, but the idea itself ran counter to the underlying assumptions of the empirical schools of psychology, philosophy, and linguistics of the first half of this century.

COGNITIVE STRUCTURALISM

But a new paradigm, which we might refer to as Cognitive Structuralism, has emerged to change the situation radically. Deeply rooted in the work of

---

[4]See Harris, 1951.

both Jean Piaget and Noam Chomsky and extending in differing directions and at times on the basis of differing secondary assumptions, the new paradigm accepts as three of its basic premises that (1) there is a realm of thought or cognitive structure separate from behavior, which mediates between our perceptions of external phenomena and our reactions to them, in which we represent to ourselves information about the world, process that information and plan our actions; (2) that this realm of cognitive structure develops in interaction with inputs from the environment but under constraints, which at some level of specificity have been preprogrammed by genetic factors;[5] and (3) that this realm of cognitive structure is separate from language, beginning its development in the child before the advent of language, providing in fact the cognitive basis upon which the child acquires language, and although perhaps later coming to be influenced and elaborated by language, continuing to serve as the structural medium in which thinking takes place. For the Cognitive Structuralists, this realm of cognitive structure cannot be ignored, shunted aside as equivalent to linguistic structure, or simply regarded as empirically impenetrable, but must in fact become the primary focus of theoretical and experimental attention, if the study of mind and behavior are to progress.

Once one grants that there exists a realm of cognitive structure that in fact provides the foundations for language acquisition, then it seems reasonable to suppose that the structural constraints inherent in that realm might be reflected in the processes by which languages are acquired and in the structures of the languages which come to be learned. So for the psychologist the search for universals in the processes of language acquisition and the search for universals in language structure emerge as potential avenues for gaining insight into the structural constraints inherent in that cognitive realm.[6] The linguist for his part gains the benefit and/or burden of a new criterion for guiding and judging his descriptive work. He can henceforth ask, not only "Is my description of a language accurate, maximally

---

[5]If Piaget is correct, there is an important degree of continuity but little specificity in the genetically-based cognitive structuring principles that pervade the development and later organization of all domains of knowledge. If Chomsky (1957, 1959, 1968, 1975), Katz (1972, with Postal, 1964), and Fodor (1975) are correct, in some domains and especially in the areas of syntactic and semantic knowledge, there is evidence of genetic preprogramming of a more differentiated and domain-specific sort. If Piaget is correct, the interaction of biologicaly preprogrammed structural proclivities with environmental inputs leads the child through a sequence of qualitatively distinct stages of cognitive structural development. If Brown (1973) and Kohlberg (1969, 1971) are correct, these progressive qualitative achievements in general cognitive structural development act as formative preconditions to developmental stage sequences in more specific content domains, such as, respectively, syntactic abilities and moral thought. See also Brewer (1974) and Chapter 2.

[6]See, among others, Brown, 1973; Chomsky, 1975; Macnamara, 1977; Slobin, 1979, Chapter 3.

generalized and maximally parsimonious?'' but also ''Do the form and categories of my description correspond with the underlying cognitive structures on the basis of which language is acquired by the child?''[7]

In addition, however, it seems likewise reasonable to suppose that if there exist cognitive structures separate from language, then just as those structures might affect and hence be reflected in language, so might language affect and hence be reflected in them. The Cognitive Structuralist paradigm, in other words, lays the theoretical infrastructure necessary for serious consideration of Whorf's claims. As language is acquired, does it necessarily take the form of a distinct, isolated set of skills that serve us exclusively as a means for communicating our thoughts, or might language in fact act to shape the underlying cognitive structures in which we think? Once language has been acquired, does it necessarily represent merely a code system, such as the Morse code, into which we translate our thoughts to communicate them, or might language transcend its purely communicative role, to become in fact a supplementary cognitive tool? If our cognitive lives and even our linguistic lives are genetically preprogrammed in certain very general ways, is it not reasonable to suppose that processes of natural selection may have encouraged the development of a species that not only communicates by language, but that has the genetic potential for taking advantage of its language for enriching the scope and facilitating the employment of its thoughts? Is it not reasonable to suppose, in other words, that despite an obvious need for qualification and greater precision, Whorf may have been on the right track?

This book can certainly not provide conclusive answers to these questions, but it is hoped that it will undercut the assumption that they are unworthy of consideration and provide some direction to continuing efforts to resolve them. Chapter 1 reports on a five year investigation into the impact of specific aspects of the English and Chinese languages on their speakers' cognitive lives,[8] and Chapter 2 draws upon the results of that investigation to build a more general model of the role languages seem to play in the development and functioning of thought. It seems appropriate to begin this exploration into the Whorfian side of the language and thought issue with the paragraph with which Dan Slobin concludes his discussion of language and cognition in his recent edition of *Psycholinguistics* (1979):

> The fate of the Sapir–Whorf hypothesis at the present time is interesting: today we are more concerned with linguistic universals and cultural universals than with linguistic and cultural relativity. Chomsky has suggested that Whorf was too much concerned with surface structures of languages, while on their deeper levels all languages are of the same universally human character. Cultural an-

---

[7]See Chomsky, 1965.
[8]See also Bloom 1979a, 1979b.

thropologists are looking for ways in which the underlying structures of cultures are alike, and psychologists are moving out of Western culture to cross-cultural studies, in an attempt to understand general laws of human behavior and development. Perhaps in an age when our world has become so small, and the most diverse cultures so intimately interrelated in matters of war and peace, it is best that we come to an understanding of what all people have in common. But at the same time it would be dangerous to forget that different languages and cultures may indeed have important effects on what people will believe and what they will do [p. 185].

1

The Distinctive Cognitive Legacies of English and Chinese

In 1972-1973, while I was in Hong Kong working on the development of a questionnaire designed to measure levels of abstraction in political thinking,[1] I happened to ask Chinese-speaking subjects questions of the form, "If the Hong Kong government were to pass a law requiring that all citizens born outside of Hong Kong make weekly reports of their activities to the police, how would you react?"; or "If the Hong Kong government had passed such a law, how would you have reacted?". Rather unexpectedly and consistently, subjects responded "But the government hasn't;" "It can't;" or "It won't." I attempted to press them a little by explaining, for instance, that "I know the government hasn't and won't, but let us imagine that it does or did . . . " Yet such attempts to lead the subjects to reason about things that they knew could not be the case only served to frustrate them and tended to give rise to such exclamations as "We don't speak/think that way;" "It's unnatural;" "It's unChinese." Some subjects with substantial exposure to Western languages and culture even branded these questions and the logic they imply as prime examples of "Western thinking." By contrast, American and French subjects, responding to similar questions in their native languages, never seemed to find anything unnatural about them and in fact readily indulged in the counterfactual hypothesizing they were designed to elicit.

The unexpected reactions of the Chinese subjects were intriguing, not only because of the cross-cultural cognitive differences they suggested, but also because the Chinese language does not have structures equivalent to those

---

[1]See Bloom, 1977a, 1977b.

through which English and other Indo-European languages mark the counterfactual realm. Could having or not having a counterfactual construction in one's language play a significant role in determining how inclined one will be to think in counterfactual terms? Could, in other words, counterfactual thinking constitute an example of an area of cognitive activity in which language-specific structures have an important impact on cognitive life? Over the past five years, I returned to East Asia three times to examine exactly what it is that the Chinese do and do not say in a counterfactual vein and to explore what the cognitive implications of these linguistic habits might be.

English, like other Indo-European languages, has distinct linguistic structures designed to signal entry into the counterfactual realm—to invite the reader or listener explicitly to shunt aside reality considerations in order to consider a state of affairs known to be false, not for the purpose of simply pretending, but for the express purpose of drawing implications as to what might be or might have been the case if that state of affairs were in fact true. When referring to the present or future, English speakers signal that shift by making use of the past form[2] of the verb or the phrase "were to" in the first clause of an otherwise straightforward implicational sentence, followed by the form "would" or " 'd" in its second clause—e.g., "If he could, he would," "If he ran faster, he would win," "If she came, I'd bake a cake," "If I were/was he, I'd respond to that letter," and "If John were to go to the library, he would see Mary." And when referring to the past, English speakers signal an equivalent shift into the realm of the counterfactual by making use of the past perfect tense in the first clause of an implicational sentence followed by the forms "would have" or "might have" in its second clause—e.g., "If John had gone to the library, he would have seen Mary," "If he hadn't run so quickly, he wouldn't have been able to stop himself before he crashed through that glass door," "Had China invaded Swat, Pakistan might have reacted violently," In French, the counterfactual realm is marked in the present by the imperfect in the first clause and the conditional in the second; in the past, by the *plus-que-parfait* in the first clause and the past conditional in the second; in Spanish, by the subjective followed by the conditional; in German by subjectives in each clause. And in each of these languages in whatever manner the counterfactual is marked, its use signals a contrast with both (1) a straightforward descriptive recounting of facts (e.g., John went to the library and saw Mary; John didn't go to the library and didn't see Mary; John goes to the library every

---

[2]Except in the case of the verb "to be," where the old subjunctive form "were" is used, barring some colloquial dialects, where by generalization the past form "was" is used. The marking of the counterfactual in the first clause is disappearing in some dialects, but, its marking in the second clause remains stable.

day and sees Mary; John will go to the library tomorrow and will see Mary) and (2) a straightforward description of an implicational relationship holding between two events that carries no commitment as to the truth or falsehood of the original premise (e.g., If John goes to the library, he will see Mary; If John went to the library, he saw Mary; If John didn't go, he certainly didn't see Mary—by contrast to "If he were to go, he would see Mary," "If he had gone, he would have seen Mary"; "If he hadn't gone, he wouldn't have passed the exam.")

A straightforward implicational sentence can be uttered with varying presuppositions as to how likely it is that the event described in its first clause or premise has or will in fact happen. One might presuppose that John went to the library and state in an almost rhetorical way, "If he *went*, he saw Mary" as if one were about to add "and that is all there is to it!" Or one might have no notion of whether or not John went, how likely the premise of the implication, and simply state "If he went, he saw Mary." Or, more atypically, one might think in fact that John is unlikely to have gone and yet state, just for the purpose of getting the reasoning straight, "*If* he went, he saw Mary." But whatever the presupposition, the use of an implicational sentence as opposed to a counterfactual one, has the effect of signaling that the statement is intended as a description of a relationship between events rather than as a summons to the listener to shift from the realm of empirical generalization to the realm of hypothetical postulation.

A grammatical analysis of Chinese, confirmed by interviewing of both Chinese monolingual speakers and native Chinese, Chinese-English bilinguals, yields a very different picture of how Chinese treats implicational and counterfactual sentences. In certain respects, Chinese speakers in everyday speech express implicational relationships in more differentiated terms than English speakers do. In the first place, while English speakers use only context and/or intonation to indicate how likely they feel it is that the premise of an implicational statement has in fact taken place, Chinese speakers make use of a much more precise linguistic device to signal the specific presupposition they intend—namely alternative forms of the word "if."[3] For example, the use of the word "chia ju" for "if" in the sentence "If the Mongols invaded Swat, they conquered it" suggests that the speaker believes that the Mongols are unlikely to have invaded that kingdom, while at the same time making clear that if they did invade, they conquered it. By contrast, an alternative form "ju kuo" expresses an implicational relation between invading and conquering, without committing the speaker to any belief about the likelihood that the invasion has in fact taken place. Secondly English speakers do not normally differentiate between "if-then" and "if-and-only-if-then" interpretations of implicational sentences. For example,

---

[3]See Chao, 1968, 116-119.

the English sentence "If China conquers Swat, it will acquire a new summer resort" leaves ambiguous whether this is the only means by which China could acquire such a resort (the if-and-only-if interpretation) or whether, in fact, there is a chance that China might acquire one by some other means; while the equivalent Chinese sentence, by making use of alternative forms of the word "then" ("ts'ai" [only if-then] vs "chiu" [then])makes the distinction clear. Yet, despite Chinese grammatical precision in expressing both the degree of likelihood of the premise of implicational statements and the distinction between if-then and if-and-only-if-then interpretations of the relationship of the premise to its consequence, the Chinese language has no distinct lexical, grammatical, or intonational device to signal entry into the counterfactual realm, to indicate explicitly that the events referred to have definitely not occurred and are being discussed for the purpose only of exploring the might-have-been or the might-be.

By itself, the fact that Chinese has no such linguistic device cannot, of course, be taken to imply anything about the way Chinese speakers think. The fact that English does not have a distinct word for check meaning "financial draft" does not mean that we confuse that kind of check with the mark next to a correct answer or with the end-game in chess. But in the particular case of the Chinese counterfactual, there was some rather compelling evidence to suggest that the lack of a distinct linguistic device to signal counterfactual thought might have cognitive consequences.[4]

In the first place, Chinese speakers, in marked contrast to their American and French counterparts, in response to the original questionnaire, had refused to shift into the counterfactual realm and, in fact, had branded questions that called upon them to do so characteristically unChinese. And, in fact, native Chinese speakers regularly report the same observation that there is something unChinese about counterfactual talk and thought. One Chinese student at Swarthmore labeled it "evil"; a professor of English at Taiwan National University remarked, "You know, we Chinese are not used to using the counterfactual as you Americans are—when I try to speak in class that way, my students quickly become confused." Bilinguals report that they feel perfectly comfortable using counterfactual statements in English such as "If the lecture had ended earlier, Bill would have had a chance to prepare for the exam," but that they feel more comfortable converting such statements into descriptive alternatives such as "The lecture ended too late, so Bill did not have a chance to prepare for the exam" in order to express the same ideas naturally in Chinese; and native Chinese, Chinese-English bilinguals who were presented with matched pairs of English counterfactual and descriptive statements and asked, for each pair,

---

[4]I am particularly indebted to Professors Heng Hsiung- jeng, Mei Guang and Benjamin K. T'sou; Gu Wan-ch'ing and Pi T'ang Chin-ch'ung for their contributions to the experimental research.

if either of the pair seems closer to the way such facts are expressed in Chinese, consistently selected the descriptive forms as the one that "captures the way we say, think about such things in Chinese." Ironically, it is in fact Westerners who have had little experience in the Chinese language and culture who are usually the most reluctant to believe that there could be something unChinese about the counterfactual, while the Chinese themselves with few exceptions readily and cheerfully confirm that it is the case.

Moreover, if the lack of a distinct marking for the counterfactual in Chinese were merely a linguistic fact, with no further cognitive consequences for speakers of Chinese, one might expect that the Chinese equivalent of the sentence "If John went to the library he saw Mary," since it would have to carry both the implicational and counterfactual interpretations (i.e., "If he had gone, he would have . . . " and "If he went, he saw . . . "), would be perceived as ambiguous by Chinese subjects, just as the sentence "Everyone loves his wife" is perceived as ambiguous by English speakers, at least once the ambiguity is pointed out. Yet the large majority of monolingual Chinese subjects interviewed did not perceive such sentences as ambiguous nor, when the two interpretations were pointed out, was there that ready click of comprehension of the distinction which is evident among speakers of Western languages under similar circumstance. In fact, after a week of working with sample sentences, my highly intelligent, monolingual research assistant was still encountering considerable difficulty in maintaining clearly in mind the idea of a counterfactual interpretation as distinct from a negative implicational one (i.e., "If he had/had not gone" vs "If he didn't go"). In effect, for the monolingual Chinese speakers interviewed, coming to recognize the distinction between counterfactual and implicational sentences seemed not to be just a question of associating new formal terms with already explicitly developed modes of categorizing experience, but rather a question of building new cognitive schemas to fit those formal terms, parallel perhaps to the predicament of the English-speaking student of logic who has to build new cognitive schemas in order to come to recognize the distinctions carried by the formal labels "if-then," "if-and-only-if-then" and "only-if-then".

Furthermore, Chinese students of English find the counterfactual to be one of the most difficult aspects of the English language to master—a fact that has been confirmed by, among others, two professors of English from Taiwan National University, many bilinguals, and several incidents such as one that took place at a conference at Rutgers a few years ago. While I was discussing my research at dinner, a professor of Chinese literature from Taiwan, who had been in the United States for about three years, suddenly interrupted the discussion to exclaim "One second, what does 'would have' mean? It is the one aspect of English grammar I have been unable to grasp!"

An informal content analysis of a leading Chinese newspaper in Taiwan conducted over a three week period uncovered only one example of the use of what one might call counterfactual argument, expressed by the circumlocution: "*X* is not the case; but if *X* then *Y*," and that turned out to be in a translation of a speech by Henry Kissinger.

Mao did tend to make use of counterfactual reasoning and to express it in this way even though he did not speak any Western languages. But he was certainly heavily influenced by Western political writings; and it is interesting to note that while Westerners find Mao's writings relatively easier to read than typical Chinese prose, and his logic relatively more accessible, I have been told on repeated occasions by people with extensive experience in mainland China that, for the Chinese, the opposite is very much the case.

Finally, a good friend of mine who was teaching Chinese in the Albany area was called to a New York State court to serve as a translator for a Taiwanese citizen who had overstayed his visa, but who had made plans to leave the country the next day. The judge asked my friend to translate the sentence, "If you weren't leaving tomorrow, you would be deportable." After struggling for a few minutes to formulate an adequate translation, she attempted to make sense out of the sentence in Chinese in a form roughly equivalent to "I know you are leaving tomorrow, but if you do not leave, you will be deported." The Taiwanese replied in Chinese, "But what do you mean? I'm leaving tomorrow. Don't worry, I'm leaving." My friend persisted in her attempts to convey the counterfactual/theoretical intent of the judge's statement, but the Taiwanese continued to interpret the statement, no matter what form the translation took, as a threat, roughly equivalent to "If you don't go, you will be deported" and so, continued to declare defensively that he was indeed leaving. Then the judge asked, "If you have to be deported, where would you wish to be deported to?", making a further cognitive leap into the realm of the pure hypothetical. Again several attempts at translation, this time with even less success. Perceiving that the Taiwanese was totally unable to comprehend what was going on and that he was, as a consequence, becoming more and more frustrated, my friend counseled him to respond "Taiwan." He did. The proceedings terminated and were recorded in the court record.[5] The Taiwanese left the country the next day apparently never understanding that it was not that the judge questioned the sincerity of his intent to leave and was therefore threatening him, but rather that the judge wanted him to understand the implications of what would happen if he did not act as he had already planned to.

Not only then does Chinese not mark the counterfactual, but Chinese speakers tend to brand the counterfactual as in some sense unChinese. They

---

[5]Immigration and Naturalization Service, Eastern Region, Buffalo District, Albany, N.Y. sub-office, 7/15/78. I am indebted to Susan Blader for this anecdote.

tend not to recognize the distinction between counterfactual and implicational statements as a division of reality with which they are familiar, and they tend to be relatively disinclined, at least by comparison to their English-speaking counterparts, to make use of counterfactual logic in responding to questionnaire queries, in writing newspaper analyses and in interpreting the implications of at least one legal situation.

Yet this evidence, suggesting a link between language and thought in the area of the counterfactual, cannot be taken to imply a complete absence of the counterfactual from the Chinese psycholinguistic world, for the Chinese, in particular in concrete situations, do make use of counterfactual speech and thought. Imagine, for example, a situation in which a group of people have been waiting for John. He arrives late and they are, as a result, late for the movies. Under such circumstances, one can say in Chinese, "If John come + past earlier, they arrive at the movies on time" and mean in English, "If John had come earlier, they would have (but didn't) arrive at the movies on time." In a situation in which a child has just taken off on his own across a street and just missed being hit by a car, his mother, having observed the incident, can say in Chinese, "If you are + past hit by the car, what do we do?" and mean in English, "If you had been hit by the car, what would we do?" Faced with an accident of which the speaker and listener are both well aware, the speaker can say in Chinese, "If he warn + past them earlier, perhaps that accident is able to be avoided" and mean in English, "If he had warned them earlier, that accident could perhaps have been avoided."[6] A Chinese speaker can state in Chinese, "Luckily John reserved a room" and then continue "if not, [(yao) pu jan (te hua)] John slept on the street" and mean "If John hadn't, he would have slept on the street." In each case, if the presupposition were different the identical sentence would have straightforward implicational meaning. If the hearer does not know that John is late, the sentence "If John come + past earlier, they arrive at the movies on time" will mean "If John came earlier, they arrived at the movies on time." If the hearer does not know whether the accident was in fact averted, the sentence, "If he warn + past them, perhaps the accident is able to be avoided" will mean "If he warned them, perhaps the accident was avoided" and if the hearer does not know whether John reserved a room, then the sentence "If not, he slept on the street" will mean "If John didn't make a reservation, he slept on the street." But within a concrete situational context which negates its premise, each of these sentences can be used to express a counterfactual thought, even though there is no explicit linguistic marking in the sentence to signal that it is to be understood in that way.

We are left then with an apparent contradiction. On the one hand, Chinese certainly do, within certain situations, think and speak counter-

---

[6] See Chao, 1968, 116.

factually; on the other, the lack of a distinct marking for the counterfactual seems, based on the evidence presented above, to be associated with significant cognitive consequences. To attempt to resolve this apparent contradiction, let us suppose that a language, by whether it labels or does not label any specific mode of categorizing experience, cannot determine whether its speakers will think that way, but can either encourage or not encourage them to develop a labeled cognitive schema specific to that mode of thought. Even if the English language did not label the notion "bachelor," English speakers could still understand the concept "bachelor" by bringing together in their minds its component elements—unmarried, never previously married, male and adult. But the fact that the English language has a distinct label for bachelor seems to encourage its speakers to develop a schema specifically designed to categorize the world in that way; and, thereby, to come to be able (1) to make and understand direct reference to bachelors and in fact to think directly about bachelors, without having to expend the cognitive effort necessary to integrate and keep simultaneously in mind the four dimensions—male, unmarried, never previously married and adult; (2) to recognize "bachelors" as one of those categories of things (in this case, individuals) into which their cognitive world is divided; and, (3) to utilize the category "bachelor" as a mode of cognitive organization in memory to which information can be attached that is not true of adults, males, unmarried people or never married people taken separately and to utilize it as a point of mental orientation for undertaking analyses for which it may serve as a convenient variable.

Long before the English-speaking child enters first year logic, she knows that her mother's statement, "If you don't carry the vase with two hands, you will break it" does not imply that there are no other ways in which she could break the glass—e.g., by letting it drop intentionally. She also knows from experience, that her mother's statement, "If you don't eat dinner, you won't get a bedtime story," by contrast, implies that there is no way, other than by eating dinner, to get a bedtime story. In other words, long before the child has command of the labels "if-then" and "if-and-only-if-then" she can think in terms of the distinction involved. But it is likely that it is not until she is exposed to those labels that she will develop cognitive schemas specifically designed to categorize the world in those ways and hence come to be able (1) to make and understand reference to, and even to think about, the distinctions involved directly, as separate from the situations in which they become manifest; (2) to recognize the distinctions as ways in which her own cognitive world is divided and (3) to make use of the distinctions as active points of mental orientation for evaluating, for example, the logical consistency of an argument.

Analogously, the fact that the English speaker has a distinct label for the counterfactual (i.e. "had . . . would have"), which the Chinese speaker does not share, cannot by any means be expected to bestow upon the English speaker an exclusive facility for that mode of thought, but it might be expected to encourage him or her, by contrast to his or her Chinese counterpart, to develop a cognitive schema specific to that way of thinking—a schema that represents an achieved integration of the idea of an implication linking two events with the idea that neither of these events constitutes a factual occurrence.

Under such an interpretation, even though the Chinese speaker does not have at his disposal a labeled schema specific to counterfactual thought he will still, upon hearing the sentence "If John come + past earlier, they get + past to the movies on time," and knowing that John didn't come earlier, interpret it counterfactually, by integrating the negating facts he knows (John didn't arrive earlier) with the stated implication (if he did, they arrived on time). But, by contrast to his English-speaking counterpart, to be sure that the sentence is counterfactual, the Chinese speaker must either be aware of the situational facts that negate its premise or be able to infer them, for there is no mark within the sentence which signals it as such. And to interpret the sentence as counterfactual, the Chinese speaker, again by contrast to his English-speaking counterpart, must perform an act of cognitive integration, integrating his knowledge of the facts of the situation with the stated premise, for his language does not convey the counterfactual directly nor has it, as a result, prepared him for interpreting it directly—i.e., for interpreting directly as a single unit the integration of a negated premise and an implication based upon it. When the English speaker hears the sentence "If you had warned them earlier, perhaps the accident would have been avoided," he is left with the cognitive burden of having to resolve what kind of warning might have been effective, how effective it is likely to have been, how responsible he personally should feel for the fact that the warning was not given, etc.; but he is not left with the burden of having to resolve that the sentence is counterfactual. The labels "had . . . would have" signal to him directly and unambiguously that a counterfactual interpretation is intended. And his language has already prepared him, through its use of those labels, to interpret directly, as a single unit, without requiring any further cognitive act, the integration of negated premise and implication based upon it. For the English speaker, the counterfactuality of a sentence constitutes, as it were, one of the elementary components on the basis of which he constructs his interpretation of the sentence heard, while for the Chinese speaker, it constitutes one of the results of his interpretive act.

In sum, then, the suggestion that Chinese speakers have not been led by their language to construct schemas specific to counterfactual speech and thought would not imply that Chinese speakers cannot speak and think counterfactually and hence would not be contradicted by evidence that they do. Such a suggestion would imply, however, that they would typically do so less directly, with a greater investment of cognitive effort and hence less naturally than their English-speaking counterparts. It would imply as well that they would not typically perceive the distinction between counterfactual and implicational (i.e., e.g., the distinction between "if he had gone...he would have seen" and "if he went...he saw") as one of the divisions into which their cognitive world is divided. It would imply that Chinese speakers might be expected typically to encounter difficulty in extending the use of counterfactual speech outside of those concrete situational contexts in which the negating facts are known or can be inferred to abstract contexts in which expressing a counterfactual thought involves not only stipulating an implication, but, in addition, explicitly and consciously stipulating the negating facts which render it counterfactual (making explicit use, for example, of the two sentence construction "China did not go through that stage. But if it did, then . . . " to express the notion "If China had gone through that stage, then..."); just as the English student who has not yet developed a labeled schema specific to if-then vs. if-and-only-if-then, while dealing comfortably with that distinction in concrete situations, has difficulty extending its use to those situations which require its explicit utilization. And, finally, the suggestion that Chinese speakers do not typically make use of cognitive schemas specific to counterfactual thought would imply that Chinese speakers might be expected typically to encounter difficulty in maintaining a counterfactual perspective as an active point of orientation for guiding their cognitive activities. Chinese speakers might be expected, for example, if presented with an extended string of complex counterfactual arguments, to find it difficult to keep in mind, as they process the complex entailment relationships which hold between the arguments presented, the fact that all the arguments concern the "would have been" or the "might have been" rather than the world of actual fact.[7]

The evidence presented so far supports this general interpretation, but to put it to a more objective test, the following experimental procedures were designed:

In an initial exploratory study, stories were prepared of the form X was not the case, but if X had been the case, then Y would have been the case, Z would have been the case, and W would have been the case, etc.—e.g., a specific Greek philosopher was unable to speak Chinese. But if he had been able to, he would have done Y, Z, W, etc.—expressed in Chinese, for lack of a way to express the counterfactual directly, as "X was not the case; but if X was, then Y, then Z, then W, etc.", in other words, in the way that the counterfactual is expressed when it is expressed in Chinese outside of the more usual concrete situational contexts, as in Mao's writings or the

---

[7]I am especially indebted to Margaret H. Bloom for her many crucial, conceptual contributions to the development of this interpretation.

translation of the Kissenger quote.[8] Subjects were then asked in a variety of direct and indirect ways whether they interpret the paragraphs as indicating that the final consequent or consequents of the series of implications presented refer to things that have happened or rather to things that have not.

English speakers, equipped with counterfactual schemas, might be expected upon seeing the words, "if he had . . . would have," to shift promptly into the counterfactual mode of processing and hence to understand in an almost self-evident manner that, of course, the consequents are to be interpreted as counterfactual, as considerations of what might have been but wasn't.[9] But, if the average Chinese speaker has not, as a result of the particular features of his language, been led to develop an already prepared interpretive framework designed for categorizing and thinking about the world in a counterfactual way, then he might be expected upon reading the paragraphs to encounter greater difficulty than would his English-speaking counterpart in recognizing the logical juxtaposition "X was not the case; but if X was, then" as an indication that the paragraph is about the realm of the might-have-been; and even if he does recognize the counterfactual import of that juxtaposition, to encounter greater difficulty than would his English-speaking counterpart in holding a counterfactual perspective in mind as a stable point of mental orientation from which to analyze the series of consequents presented. The central question is, in other words, to what extent Chinese subjects will impose a counterfactual interpretation on a paragraph which expresses a complex abstract counterfactual argument in the way that such an argument is expressed when it is expressed in Chinese?

In the case of this paragraph, as well as the other written experimental manipulations described below, a great many distinct forms of expression were used during pre-testing to control for the possibility that the specific expressions used were prejudicing the results found. Almost every word-change had some marginal effect in one way or the other, but no alternative form produced results which in any way contradict the principal thrust of the data presented.

Chinese versions of the stories were presented during the summer of 1975 to a group of hotel workers in Taiwan as well as to a group of students at Taiwan National University, the college of highest prestige in Taiwan. English versions were presented as a control to a group of students at Swarthmore College, U.S.A. during the fall of the same year.

---

[8]See Appendix A for sample texts and response formats.

[9]It should be noted that the counterfactual mode of processing, psychologically speaking, is not equivalent to the formal logical mode of processing a statement such as Not X, X, $\longrightarrow Y$. In counterfactual talk/thought, use of the terms "If X had . . . Y would have . . ." necessarily implies that Y did not occur; while, in purely logical terms, if X is linked to Y by a unidirectional implication, the fact that X is untrue does not necessarily imply anything about the truth or falsity of Y.

The results of this preliminary study were rather dramatic. At Swarth-more, 25 out of the 28 or 89% of the students tested consistently responded that the events referred to in the last statements of the stories were false—that is, imposed counterfactual interpretations on the paragraphs; and the remaining three students gave only one inconsistent response each, which on the basis of later interviewing, turned out to be attributable to am-biguity with regard to the if vs. if-and-only-if distinction, rather than to am-biguity with regard to the counterfactual distinction. Among the 54 Chinese students tested, all of whom had some exposure to English and some of whom had very considerable exposure to English, 37 or 69% made con-sistently counterfactual responses; finally, among the working class sub-jects, who had little exposure to English, the number of consistent counter-factual responders drops to 6 out of 36 or 17%. In later interviewing, the Chinese subjects who had missed the counterfactual import of the paragraphs indicated either (1) that by the time they had gotten to the last few implications in the series, they had forgotten that the philosopher could not speak Chinese and so evaluated those later implications as statements of what he in fact had done; or (2), and this was the case for the large majority of subjects—that they had remembered the philosopher could not speak Chinese but had found that fact in contradiction to the statements in the rest of the paragraphs and so, in order to salvage as much as possible, had decided that what must be intended was at least that the philosopher had done X, Y, Z and W. Otherwise, why write about it? In other words, for the majority of Chinese-speaking subjects tested, although recognition of the juxtaposition of a negative premise and implicational statements based upon it did lead to the realization that something was askew, it did not trig-ger, as it did in the West, a counterfactual interpretation.

The results, furthermore, speak not only to the absence of a schema cor-responding to the English and Indo-European counterfactual among the majority of Chinese speakers, but also to the specific relevance of linguistic variables to that fact. Degree of training in English was positively and significantly correlated with ability to grasp and work successfully in the counterfactual mode, as measured by the task, among the working subjects at the .01 level and the student subjects at the .05 level. It was, moreover, in fact the case that many of the Chinese subjects who responded correctly wrote the words "would have" in English in the margin of the stories they were reading, even though the questionnaire was written in Chinese and distributed by a Chinese research assistant. There was no reason for these subjects to suspect that anyone capable of reading English might be reading their responses, other than perhaps the fact that if they grasped the counter-factual logic of the paragraphs, it might have suggested to them that Westerners were in some way involved; yet they used the English words "would have" as if those English words helped them to maintain a conscious involvement in the counterfactual mode of thought, as if those words insured the continued activation of a schema, drawn from their English repertory, which would, in this case, be helpful in processing Chinese.

Two years later, as part of a broader study, an effort was made to test again and, in somewhat more precise terms, the extent to which Chinese speakers as compared to their Western counterparts, would indulge, outside of concrete situational contexts, in counterfactual reasoning. Two new versions of the original paragraph were prepared and distributed to Chinese-speaking subjects in Taiwan and Hong Kong and to English-speaking subjects in the U.S.A. Like the original, both new versions (Versions Two and Three) talk about "X not being the case, but if X, then Y" and so, from a Western perspective at least, call for counterfactual interpretations. But the content of Version Two allows the subject to make sense out of the paragraph even if he does not invoke a counterfactual interpretation (although a different sense, contradictory to the one he would infer on the basis of a counterfactual interpretation); while, by contrast, the content of Version Three makes it logically impossible to come up with any coherent interpretation of the paragraph at all unless one invokes a counterfactual interpretation. More specifically, both versions begin with the statements (1) that Bier was an Eighteenth Century German philosopher who wanted to investigate the principles of the universe and the laws of nature and (2) that works of Chinese philosophy were to be found in Europe because at that time relatively frequent contact existed between China and Europe. But the second version then goes on to state that only a very few Chinese philosophical works had been translated while the third asserts that none had been translated. Both versions then continue alike in stating that Bier couldn't read Chinese, but if he had been able to, he would have discovered the relevance to his own work of certain Chinese philosophical works, would have been influenced by them and would have, as a result, gone on to develop a new integrative philosophical theory that would have overcome an important weakness in Western philosophical thought of that time and have brought Western philosophy closer to science. Of course, there is no way in Chinese to express "had been" or "would have" directly and so what is expressed in Chinese is roughly equivalent to "He couldn't read Chinese, but if he could he discovered . . . was influenced by . . . etc." But the question at issue is again whether Chinese speakers, despite the lack of a linguistic means to mark the counterfactual, will still impose a counterfactual integration on a juxtaposition of a negated premise and an implication based upon it, whether their cognitive behavior reflects a mode of categorizing the world which their language doesn't mark.

In Version Two, if a subject comes upon the sentence "Bier couldn't speak Chinese; but if he could . . . " and sees no immediate way of making sense out of the apparent logical inconsistency contained within it, he can easily dismiss the contradiction as some incorrect quirk of phrasing and still arrive at a coherent interpretation of the paragraph. Bier couldn't read Chinese, but since some translations were available, the fact that he couldn't read Chinese would, logically speaking, not have necessarily prevented Bier from gaining access to Chinese works, from being influenced by them, hence from developing a new integrative theory, etc. Such an interpretation, once formed, is likely, moreover, to be perceived from a Chinese perspective as highly acceptable for, if the paragraph is not about what Bier did, why write it at all?

In Version Three, however, if the subject misses the structural call for the counterfactual and hence proceeds by attempting to construct a straightforward descriptive interpretation of the paragraph, he soon runs up against an irreconcilable logical conflict that he cannot resolve in a coherent manner without adopting a counterfactual interpretation. Bier could not read Chinese but, in this instance, no translations were available, so how within the limits imposed by the paragraph itself, could Bier have had access to Chinese works, been influenced by them, etc., how could the paragraph be talking about what happened? While the second version, then, allows the subject to finesse the counterfactual issue and come up with a straightforward descriptive interpretation that lets him answer the question; the third version, its negated premise devoid of loopholes, allows for no such finesse. It rather forces a confrontation with the need for integrating a negated premise and implications based upon it and hence maximizes the chances that the Chinese speaker will make use of counterfactual logic, whether on the basis of a schema specifically designed to the task or on the basis of alternative, circumventive ones.

Version Three is likewise designed, from a purely stylistic point of view, to make the need for the use of counterfactual logic maximally salient. The third version recounts its "counterfactual" implications in a more straightforward, less elaborated and hence less distracting way than does the second version, thereby making it easier for a subject as he reads through those implications to keep in mind that they all follow from a negated premise. In addition, the third Chinese version makes use of two rather than just one instance of the word "if" and several rather than no instances of the construction "i ting hui"[10]—roughly equivalent to the English "certainly

---

[10]The Chinese auxiliary "hui" is at times roughly equivalent to the English "can" and at other times roughly equivalent to the English "might"; but it was suggested to me by several Chinese linguists and other informants that "hui," especially when coupled with "i ting" to create "certainly can/might," is vague enough in usage not to force either the unwanted "can" or "might" interpretation and yet indefinite enough to act as a potent reminder of the nonactuality of the consequences being discussed. Subjects did find the paragraphs somewhat more fluent when "i ting hui" was used, but its use did not exert any appreciable distinct effect on overall inclination to respond counterfactually. Similarly, the use of the Chinese form roughly equivalent to "if and only if then" (ts'ai) rather than the form roughly equivalent to

might.'' These changes add particular emphasis to the non-certainty, the non-actual descriptive quality of the content being expressed and thus presumably further discourage the subject from peremptory acceptance of a straightforward descriptive interpretation of the paragraph.

In broader perspective then, the new versions of the counterfactual paragraphs seek to define the limits of Chinese counterfactual responding; the second, by determining how inclined the average Chinese speaker will be to indulge in counterfactual thoughts when the cues to such an indulgence are least obvious and the means of circumvention most accessible; and the third, by determining how inclined to the counterfactual he will be when the cues become as obtrusive as possible, and when the paragraph becomes in fact impossible to interpret coherently without some appeal to counterfactual logic.

The English text of Version Two follows. See the appendix for the English text of Version Three and the Chinese texts:

Bier was an Eighteenth Century European philosopher who wanted very much to investigate the principles of the universe and the laws of nature. Because there was some contact between China and the West at that time, works of Chinese philosophy could be found in Europe, but very few had been translated. Bier could not read Chinese, but if he had been able to read Chinese, he would have discovered that those Chinese philosophical works were relevant to his own investigations. What would have most influenced him would have been the fact that Chinese philosophers, in describing natural phenomena, generally focused on the interrelationships between such phenomena, while Western philosophers by contrast generally focused on the description of such phenomena as distinct individual entities. Once influenced by that Chinese perspective, Bier would then have synthesized Western and Chinese views and created a new philosophical theory which focuses on natural phenomena both in terms of their mutual interrelationships and as individual entities. He would have overcome a weakness in Western philosophical thought of that century and, moreover, deeply influenced German, French and Dutch philosophers, encouraging Western philosophy to take a step forward and at the same time approach more closely to science.

Please indicate, by choosing *one or more* of the following answers what contribution or contributions Bier made to the West, according to the paragraph above:

1. Bier led Western philosophy to pay attention to natural phenomena as individual entities.

"if then" (chiu) in the statement of the implications did not exert any appreciable distinct effect on Chinese responses, confirming evidence obtained from interviewing that suggested that the lack of counterfactual responding among Chinese did not result from an attempt to deal in a formal logical manner with the paragraph at hand.

2. He led Western philosophy to pay attention to the mutual interrelationships among natural phenomena.
3. He led European philosophy closer to science.
4. He led Western philosophy one step closer to Chinese philosophy.
5. None of these answers are appropriate. (Please explain your own opinion briefly).

If the hypothesis is correct that Chinese speakers in general, by contrast to their English-speaking counterparts, do not have at their disposal already prepared cognitive schemas specifically designed for interpreting informa- tion in a counterfactual way, then neither in response to the second version nor in response to the third version should Chinese subjects show the kind of automatic, reflexive, virtually exceptionless counterfactual response characteristic of Western subjects. Moreover, if the distinct designs of the two versions of the paragraph are effective, then within the circumscribed range of Chinese counterfactual responding that does take place, responses to Version Two should reflect less counterfactual reasoning than Version Three, the responses to the former delimiting as it were the minimum end and, to the latter, the maximum end of the range of willingness of Chinese- speaking subjects to entertain counterfactual thoughts.

The data summarized in Table 1 strongly confirm these expectations.

As expected, American subjects display an automatic inclination to im- pose counterfactual interpretations on the paragraphs, while their Chinese counterparts do not. The group of Chinese subjects with the highest percen- tage of counterfactual responses only reaches a maximum of 63% and that group is responding to Version Three and consists of students at Taiwan National University who have received extensive training in English throughout their secondary school and university education. Combining all Chinese groups across the two versions, the average percentage of Chinese counterfactual responses is only 29% vs. 97% for Americans. The scores of each of the Chinese groups for each version differ significantly from the American scores for that version in the expected direction at at least $p <$ .0001[11] The scores for each of the Chinese groups on Version Two differ significantly from their respective scores on Version Three in the expected

---

[11]Version Two:

Taiwanese Non-students vs. Americans	$X^2_{df = 1} = 107.2, p < .0001$
Taiwanese Students vs. Americans	$X^2_{df = 1} = 70.06, p < .0001$
Hong Kong Students vs. Americans	$X^2_{df = 1} = 61.33, p < .0001$

Version Three:

Taiwanese Non-students vs. Americans	$X^2_{df = 1} = 27.07, p < .0001$
Taiwanese Students vs. Americans	$X^2_{df = 1} = 16.35, p < .0001$
Hong Kong Students vs. Americans	$X^2_{df = 1} = 22.15, p < .0001$

direction at at least P < .001.[12] Finally, the shift from Version Two to Version Three, as might be expected, has essentially no effect on American subjects, since a summons to shift into the counterfactual realm, as English-speaking subjects understand it, constitutes in effect a summons to ignore such things as whether or not translations exist. In sum, the data point rather compellingly to the conclusion that the observed linguistic differences between English and Chinese in the marking of counterfactuals are not merely differences in linguistic form, but differences in linguistic form that reflect and may very well be highly responsible for important differences in the way English speakers, as opposed to Chinese speakers, categorize and operate cognitively with the world.

Three months after Version Two of the Bier paragraph had been administered to the group of 75 non-student Taiwanese, a subgroup of 21 of that original group who, besides being native speakers of Chinese, spoke English and used it every day in business, were asked to respond to a second paragraph of similar content and equivalent design, this one written in English rather than in Chinese. The responses of this subgroup of subjects on the Chinese version had mirrored the responses of the group of 75 as a whole—in other words, about 6% had given counterfactual interpretations, while approximately 94% had given non-counterfactual ones. Since they had received no feedback on their original responses to the Chinese version and had responded overwhelmingly non-counterfactually to it, if the fact that they had already responded to a similar paragraph influenced their later taking of the English version at all, it should have influenced it in the direction of maintaining consistency and hence increasing non-counterfactual responding. Yet, while only 6% of these native-speaking Chinese subjects had responded counterfactually to the Chinese version of the paragraph, 18 out of 21 or 86% of the same subjects responded counterfactually to the equivalent paragraph written in English. The difference between their own Chinese language and English language responses are significant at $p < .0001$ ($X^2 = 58.34$), and the difference between the counterfactual response rate of this group of bilinguals responding in English and the counterfactual response rate of the comparable group of Taiwanese non-student who had responded to Chinese Version Three, rather than Version Two of the Bier paragraph, is likewise significant in the expected direction, $p < .01$ ($X^2_{df = 1} = 9.54$). At Taiwan National University, English versions of the Bier paragraph were also distributed to a randomly chosen third group of student subjects while Chinese Versions Two and

---

[12]Taiwanese Non-students: Version two vs. three: $X^2_{df = 1} = 29.69, p < .0001$
Taiwanese Students: Version two vs. three: $X^2_{df = 1} = 21.19, p < .0001$
Hong Kong Students: Version two vs. three: $X^2_{df = 1} = 8.56, p < .001$

TABLE 1

In response to *Version Two:*

Sample description	Number of Subjects	Number of counterfactual responses[1]	Percent of counterfactual responses
Taiwanese Non-students[2]	75	5	6%
Taiwanese Students[4]	28	2	7%
Hong Kong Students[5]	17	1	6%
American combined students/ non-students[6]	55	54	98%

In response to *Version Three:*

Taiwanese Non-students[3]	44	22	46%
Taiwanese Students[4]	38	24	63%
Hong Kong Students[5]	20	10	50%
American combined students/ non-students[6]	52	50	96%

[1]If the subject by choosing alternatives 2, 3 or 4, indicated that he/she interpreted the paragraph as referring to things that Bier actually did, his/her response was coded as non-counterfactual. By contrast, if the subject, by choosing alternative 5 and appropriately explaining his/her choice, indicated that, according to the paragraph, Bier couldn't speak Chinese and therefore hadn't accomplished any of the things referred to, his/her response was coded as counterfactual. The few subjects who chose alternative 1—irrelevant misreading of the paragraph—or who chose number 5, but did not justify their choice appropriately, were excluded from the analysis of this question. The use of totally open-ended response formats, in which the subject was simply asked "What contributions did Bier make, according to the above paragraph, to the advancement of Western philosophy?", as opposed to the partly open-ended alternative choice format described here, did not exert any appreciably distinct effect on subjects' responses.

[2]A sample of 75 subjects, the large majority of which were university graduates, ranging in age from 22-60, with an average age of 35; ranging in occupation from secretaries and clerks to businessmen and bank executives; approximately equally divided by sex.

[3]A sample of approximately equivalent population parameters to #2.

[4]A sample of students drawn from various departments at Taiwan National University, Taiwan's most prestigious university—with an average age of 20, approximately 2/3 female.

[5]A sample of students drawn from various departments at Hong Kong University, Hong Kong's most prestigious university; age range generally 20-24 with a few older subjects; approximately 2/3 male.

[6]A combined sample of 107 college educated non-students and students from Swarthmore College, ranging in age from 16-43, with an average age of 21, approximately 55% female.

Three were being distributed to the two other student groups. In this student sample, counterfactual response to the English version was again significantly higher than counterfactual response to the Chinese Version Two (52% vs. 7%, $X^2 = 13.72$, $p < .001$) but, as an exception to the general pattern of the data, slightly lower than counterfactual response to Chinese Version Three (52% vs. 63%) (See the following).

Finally, samples of 173 Taiwanese subjects and 115 American subjects responded in their native languages to the following question:

"If all circles were large and this small triangle

'Δ' were a circle, would it be large?"

Forty-four or 25% of the Taiwanese subjects answered "yes" by contrast to 95 or 83% of the American subjects—a difference significant at $p < .00001$ $X^2_{df = 1} = 39.80$). When the question is asked in the less abstract form, "If all chairs were red and this table were a chair, would it be red?" equivalent cross-linguistic differences arise. And, moreover, when the original question is asked orally, it produces even more dramatic results. It has been my experience in fact that when subjects are presented with the question orally and informally—in other words, without given time to hesitate, to reconsider or to examine the question from different perspectives—just about every native Chinese speaker who has not been exposed to strong Western influences, and even very many who have, will spontaneously respond "no," while, by contrast, just about every native English speaker will spontaneously respond "yes." During a talk I gave at Hong Kong University to a group of about twenty interested faculty members, I presented the question orally and, to a person, the audience divided along native speaker lines. Most Chinese respond "No! How can a circle be a triangle? How can this small circle be large? What do you mean?" Others elaborate further, as did a rather skeptical Chinese friend of mine with the following comment: "I know what you Westerners want me to do, you always want me to assume things, even when they don't make sense. But we Chinese don't do that." Americans for their part generally accept without question both the counterfactual premise that all circles are large and the counterfactual and, in fact, counter-logical premise that a specific triangle is a circle, despite its obvious inherent logical inconsistency, and then go on to reason within the counterfactual world thus created. Invocation of their counterfactual schema seems, as it were, to both permit and legitimize that indulgence.

Again, as in the case of the Bier paragraphs, bilingual Chinese speakers responding to an English language version of this question demonstrated greater readiness to entertain a counterfactual interpretation than did Chinese subjects of comparable age, sex and education who responded to the Chinese language version. Only 44 out of 173 or 25% of the subjects who read the question in Chinese answered "yes" as compared to 30 out of 70 or 43% of the subjects who read the question in English—a difference significant at $p < .01$ ($X^2 = 7.14$). The data suggests, in other words, that for many, if not most, of the bilinguals in the study, the counterfactual mode of thought remains associated in their minds with the English linguistic world, activated more readily when cognitive processing is elicited by that linguistic world rather than by their native Chinese.

Chinese bilingual speakers, who use the counterfactual in English and who find themselves in situations which call upon them to translate abstract English arguments into Chinese, might be expected over time to begin to extend their use of the counterfactual into their Chinese linguistic world by, for example, attaching the "counterfactual" as a second meaning to their Chinese labels for "if-then." At that point, their Chinese label "if-then" would become, for them, an explicitly ambiguous signal of both the implicational and the counterfactual, and they would begin to respond as readily in Chinese as they do in English to invitations to the counterfactual realm. The group of Taiwan National University students who, as an exception to the general pattern of the data, responded with rather similar percentages of counterfactual responses to both the English and Chinese versions of the Bier paragraphs are likely, in fact, to have reached this "compound" stage,[13] especially considering the degree to which the university environment in which they live homogenizes English and Chinese and provides an impetus to translation into Chinese of highly abstract English arguments. But for most bilinguals tested, the counterfactual seems to play a role in their use of English which it does not play in their use of Chinese—a finding which adds considerable strength both to the claim that the counterfactual is less natural to Chinese and to the more general claim that at least certain uses of counterfactual reasoning may be intimately connected with linguistic knowledge, if not dependent on the presence of linguistic labels specific to them.

One could accept the evidence of an intimate link between language and thought in the counterfactual and yet argue that rather than reflecting the impact of language structure on thought, the evidence reflects the existence within Chinese society of a general cultural proclivity against counterfactual thinking which is responsible for both the lack of an explicit marking of the counterfactual in the language and the reluctance of Chinese speakers to venture into the counterfactual realm. But the very fact that the English-speaking child from the outset hears thoughts expressed in an explicitly counterfactual way and by early adolescence is expected himself to become master in both concrete and abstract contexts of explicit counterfactual speech, while his Chinese counterpart does not share this linguistic ex-

---

[13]"Compound bilingualism" refers to the situation in which the bilingual has one cognitive schema for a concept that is labeled by a distinct label in each of his languages. "Coordinate bilingualism" refers to the situation in which by contrast the bilingual has a distinct schema and a distinct label in both of his linguistic worlds (See Earle, 1967; Ervin-Tripp, 1973; Taylor, 1976, Chapter 7).

perience, must affect importantly the relative facility each develops for this mode of speech and thought—particularly so, moreover, for even though the rudiments of counterfactual thinking may predate language development, further development of a facility for counterfactual thought must take place within a language and hence be subject to whatever influence that language exerts. The child can learn independently of his language to walk or paint or even to pretend to be someone else, and so his development of these abilities is unlikely to be substantially influenced by the characteristics of his language. But postulating false premises for the express purpose of drawing implications from them about what would be the case if they were true is a psycholinguistic act. Hence development of a facility for it is likely to be highly contingent on the nature of the incentives that language provides. As the child matures, continuing exposure to cultural forms which themselves emphasize or deemphasize counterfactual logic will surely act to further encourage or discourage his use of it. But it is not in gest or music or the plastic arts that cultures express their proclivity for or against the counterfactual. It is rather in such areas as literature, mathematics, history, philosophy and socio-political analysis—in those cultural forms, in other words, which use the language of the culture as their medium of expression and which therefore are most likely themselves to bear the influence of whatever biases that language introduces into the formulation of ideas. The present argument is not that cultural proclivities do not make important contributions to the shaping of thought, but rather that linguistic structures also make their contributions and that as one moves into increasingly abstract cognitive realms, such as that of the counterfactual, the formative contributions of linguistic structures to both thought and culture become increasingly pronounced. (For a much more comprehensive discussion of this point, see Chapter 2).

THEORETICAL EXTENSIONS

Moreover, the link between language and thought in the counterfactual becomes even more interesting when one considers that it appears to constitute only one aspect of a much more general pattern of language and thought interconnections evident in the psycholinguistic habits of speakers of English and Chinese. In one sense, the counterfactual acts like any ordinary linguistic label might act in encouraging speakers of English to add one more structured perspective to the array of structured perspectives through which they ordinarily make sense out of, code and process information about the world. But in another sense, the counterfactual differs from most other linguistic elements in that it seems to constitute a member of a special set of English and, more generally, Indo-European linguistic devices that lead speakers to develop cognitive schemas specifically designed to enable and encourage them to shift from describing, questioning, or even commanding within their baseline models of reality, to projecting and operating with theoretical extractions from those baseline models. And not only does the Chinese language not have any structures equivalent to the counterfactual but neither does it have structures equivalent to the additional members of this special set of English and, more generally, Indo-European elicitors of theoretically extracted thoughts.

The Generic Concept

A child who learns English as a first language first learns to use the English article "the" to signal a particularly determined object or objects rather than just any one of a kind.[14] Then, somewhat later, the child learns to use "the" to refer to a particularly determined object only if the particularly determined object is either one of a kind (e.g., the President of the Senegal; the highest sand dune in Abu Dhabi; the first person to ski on Jupiter, etc.) or if there is some reason for the child to presuppose that his listener has some familiarity with the object referred to, either because it is actually present in the speech context, or because it has been previously mentioned or just because the child knows that his listener is already familiar with it. Even though, for example, the child may want to tell a friend about a particular dog he saw yesterday, he must start by stating, "I met a (rather than "the") dog yesterday" and then, only once his friend has gained through the child's comments some acquaintance with that dog, can the child begin to talk about "the" dog. But mastery of these complex conditions governing the use of "the" still does not constitute full mastery of the use of that English article. The child has still to learn that using "the" with singular, concrete, count nouns that do not refer to one of a kind or to any previously familiar object, in other words, using it under precisely those conditions where its use should be ungrammatical, may not be ungrammatical at all, but rather the signal of another meaning altogether. In such a case, "the" acts not to direct attention to a particular object but acts instead to direct attention to a generic concept conceptually extracted from the realm of actual or even imaginary objects. If an English speaker speaks of "the kangaroo" while standing next to a large marsupial or after just having discussed his friend's pet kangaroo, his use of "the" will be interpreted as entailing reference to the particular relevant kangaroo. But if the same speaker talks of "the kangaroo" in the absence of any actual kangaroo or previous mutual familiarity with one, "the" will no longer be interpreted as entailing reference to any particular kangaroo, but will rather be interpreted as a

---

[14]See Maratsos, 1976.

signal of the generic kangaroo—as a signal to the listener to direct his attention to a theoretical entity extracted from the world of actual kangaroos. With a herd of buffalo off in the distance, a comment like "The buffalos are disappearing" will be interpreted as entailing reference to particular vanishing beasts. But in the same context, if the speaker shifts to the singular to say "The buffalo is disappearing," since there is no vanishing buffalo that is likely to constitute the object of his reference, his use of "the" will act as a pointer, not to an actual or actual buffalos, but to the generic buffalo and to a descriptive model of the world built in terms of such theoretical entities.[15] Similarly, when the English speaker shifts from talking about "his success" or the "success of that venture" to talking about "success," or shifts from talking about "his thoughts" or "the thought that . . . " to talking about "thought," he likewise shifts from discussion of a particular instance or particular instances to discussion of a generic concept conceptually extracted from those instances. (With abstract rather than concrete nouns—the shift is signaled by the dropping of the article altogether, rather than by its use in circumstances that do not readily yield a referential interpretation.)

In Chinese, the situation is quite different. Specific demonstrative adjectives and specific quantifiers are used to denote distinctly the English "this kangaroo;" "that kangaroo;" "these kangaroos;" "one single definite or indefinite kangaroo;" "the average kangaroo;" "several kangaroos;" and "all kangaroos." The unmodified word "kangaroo" is used generally to cover the range of cases in which English would use "a kangaroo," "the kangaroo," "kangaroos" and "the kangaroos." Word order takes care of the definite/indefinite distinction so that "kangaroo/s arrived" (taishu lai le), with "kangaroo" placed before the verb, carries the meaning that the particular, definite kangaroo or kangaroos expected have arrived; while "arrived kangaroo/s" (lai le taishu), with "kangaroo" placed after the verb, carries the meaning that some unexpected, hence indefinite, kangaroo or kangaroos has/have arrived. The distinction between plural and singular usually remains unstated, to be inferred if needed from context, although it can be made clear by use of the demonstratives or quantifiers mentioned above. But Chinese does not have any direct means to specify that one is talking about a theoretical kangaroo, by contrast to a particular kangaroo or to all particular kangaroos.

One evening while I was talking in general about my work with a Chinese professor of comparative Chinese/English linguistics from Taiwan National University, he suddenly commented, "You know, English has a whole complex of ways of talking, and hence thinking, on an abstract, theoretical level, which Chinese doesn't have. We speak and think more

---

[15]See Plotkin, 1977.

directly"—a comment, by the way, I have heard again and again from others equally well qualified to judge. He then continued in a more specific vein—"For my students of English, besides the use of the counterfactual, the hardest thing to master is the use of articles—in fact, even most very good Chinese bilingual speakers cannot use articles correctly." He went on about this for a moment more, then suggested that we ask his wife, who has a very modest command of English, how she understands the Chinese phrase "kangaroo" (taishu). He gave her the Chinese sentence, "(The) kangaroo/s is/are eat turnip/s of animal/s" (Taishu shih ch'ih lopo ti tungwu) and asked her whether she understood it as talking about a singular kangaroo or plural kangaroos. From the generality of the content of the statement and the lack of any kangaroos in the vicinity or previous mention of any, she inferred that the sentence must be referring to plural kangaroos; in fact, to all kangaroos (soyu ti taishu). He then asked if it could alter- natively be talking about a conceptual kangaroo (kuannien shang ti taishu), something other than an actual or all actual kangaroos; and she replied, "What do you mean by 'conceptual' kangaroo? Either you are talking about a single kangaroo or about all kangaroos. What else is there?"

One hundred and ten Taiwanese subjects, with varying levels of English ability, were later asked whether the same sentence "Taishu shih ch'ih lopo ti tungwu," in addition to referring to an actual kangaroo, to some actual kangaroos or even to all actual kangaroos, might have an additional inter- pretation, for example, as a conceptual kangaroo. Despite the suggestive wording of the question, only 41, or 37% of the subjects, answered yes and most of those subjects had had extensive exposure to English. Perhaps the fact that English has a distinct way of marking the generic concept plays an important role in leading English speakers, by contrast to their Chinese counterparts, to develop schemas specifically designed for creating ex- tracted theoretical entities, such as the theoretical buffalo, and hence for coming to view and use such entities as supplementary elements of their cognitive worlds.[16] Further research is certainly needed on this point, but the suggestion gains greater strength when viewed in the context of addi- tional differences between English and Chinese relating to the relative in- ducements each offers its speakers for shunting aside their baseline models of reality in favor of assuming an extracted, detached theoretical perspec- tive on them.

Entification of Properties and Actions

For English speakers, the shift from "sincere" to "sincerity," from "hard"

---

[16]Extracting theoretical entities from one's baseline model is quite different from creating an imaginary entity such as a spirit, a ghost or a dragon and placing it within one's baseline model.

to "hardness," from "red" to "redness," from "important" to "importance," from "abstract" to "abstraction," and from "counterfactual" to "counterfactuality" as well as from "to further" to "the furtherance of," from "to accept" to "the acceptance of," from "to proliferate" to "the proliferation of" and from "to generalize" to "the generalization of" on one level is simply a shift from adjective to noun or from verb to noun. But on a deeper semantic level, this shift parallels the shift from "the kangaroo over there" to "the kangaroo" and from "the success of that venture" to "success," in that it signals movement from description of the world as it is primarily understood in terms of actions, properties and things, to description of the world in terms of theoretical entities that have been conceptually extracted from the speaker's baseline model of reality and granted, psychologically speaking, a measure of reality of their own. In that baseline model, things are red, hard, important or imaginary; people are sincere and arguments, abstract. People accept, discover, proliferate and generalize. But when an English speaker adds "-ity," "-ness," "-ance," "-tion," "-ment," "-age" to talk of "sincerity," "redness," "importance" and "abstraction," of "the committee's 'acceptance' of that proposal," of "John's 'discovery' of that ancient theory," of "the 'proliferation' of nuclear arms," or of "Joan's 'generalization' of the argument from one context to another," he talks of properties and actions as if they were things; he converts in effect what are in his baseline model of reality characteristics of things and acts things perform into things in themselves—and by means of such entification, ascends to a more conceptually detached way of dividing up the world.

This is not to say that all English nouns constructed out of verbs or adjectives by the addition of nominalizing suffixes have, psychologically speaking, the status of entifications of actions or properties. "Transportation," for instance, does not represent to English speakers an entification of the act of transporting, but has rather evolved into an ordinary noun that denotes the means by which the act of transporting is carried out. Likewise, when English speakers talk of "generalizations" or "discoveries," they can mean the things that have been generalized or discovered rather than the acts of discovery or generalization. "Hindrance" is usually used to refer to the result of hindering rather than to entify the act involved.[17] But English

---

[17] It seems reasonable to suppose that entified forms are created by the speaker as he needs them from their underlying adjectival or verbal forms, while nominalized forms that have come to represent things on their own are coded separately from any corresponding adjectival or verbal forms. In other words, to make use of the concept "furtherance," the speaker may call upon the schema for "to further" as well as the schema for "entification" and to make use of the concept "opacity," call upon the schema "opaque" plus the schema for "entification"; while, by contrast, to utilize the concept "transportation" or "discovery" in the ordinary nominal sense, the speaker may make use of individual nominal schemas specifically designed to those concepts, which may or may not have corresponding verbal counterparts (cf. Chomsky, 1972; Fromkin, 1973).

speakers frequently do make use of nominalizing endings, as well as of the related gerundive form (e.g., "his furthering of," "his generalizing in that way") to convert acts into things, and they do often use nominalizing endings to convert properties into things as well and, as such, take advantage of another mechanism their language provides for moving in speech and thought from reliance on the categories of their baseline model of the actual world to reliance on theoretical categories extracted from and superimposed atop that model.

In Chinese, there are innumerable examples of distinct noun forms that have evolved to capture what are in effect the means or results of actions—forms parallel, in other words, to the English terms "transportation," "generalization" in the non-entified sense and "hindrance." Since Chinese did not traditionally permit the affixation of derivational endings (e.g., "-ity," etc.), these noun forms are not constructed out of verbal forms, but constitute separate lexical items that do not necessarily resemble in sound or written form the verbs with which they are semantically related. But just as the Chinese language does not have any mechanism with which to signal the counterfactual or any mechanism with which to signal the generic concept, nor has it had at least until recent data, any mechanism with which to entify properties or actions—any mechanism by which to shift to the more theoretically extracted categorization of the world that entification entails.

Some very significant changes have been occurring in both spoken and written Chinese as a response to the pressure of Western influence. Suffixes corresponding to the English "-ize," "-ism," "-ology," "-ist" and "-itis" have emerged in the Chinese language within the relatively recent past with which Chinese speakers can now convert, for instance, "soft," "modern," and "normal" into "soften," "modernize," and "normalize"; "capital" and "Marx" into "capitalism" and "Marxism"; "society" and "language" into "sociology" and "linguistics"; "science" into "scientist" and "appendix" into "appendicitis."[18] And, as part of this influx of suffixes, forms have also emerged for converting certain adjectives into nominal counterparts. With them, Chinese speakers can now transform the adjective "possible" into a distinct form for "possibility," the adjective "serious" into a distinct form for "seriousness," the adjective "efficient" into a distinct form for "efficiency" and the adjective "important" into a distinct form for "importance." But the use of these nominalizing devices does not yet constitute a natural, freely productive aspect of Chinese grammar. Sentences employing such devices are still perceived as markedly foreign in flavor by a very large segment of the present-day Taiwanese and Hong Kong populations and, as such, are considered to be less aesthetic if, at times, unavoidable, alternatives to 'purely' Chinese adjectival forms. The

---

[18]For further discussion, see Chao, 1968, 225-228.

use of these imported nominalizing devices does not as yet generalize, as it does in Western languages, from the nominalization of adjectives to the nominalization of verbs and even within the adjectival realm itself remains tightly restricted. Certain specific forms such as those exemplified above, do have currency; but as soon as one attempts to extend the accepted set on one's own, the limits of acceptability are quickly violated. In present-day Taiwan, for example, one can shift from talking about "something being possible" to "the possibility of something" and from "something being important" to "the importance of something," but no acceptable means has yet emerged for converting "white" to "whiteness," "probable," to "probability," "subtle" to "subtlety," or "abstract" to "abstraction," much less for transforming "accept" to "acceptance," "preserve" to "preservation," "elucidate" to "elucidation" or "generalize" to "generalization."

The linguistic traditions of the past are then still far from erased; but the evidence of penetration of Western forms is itself very revealing. It both points to probable future directions of language change in Chinese and brings further confirmation to the suggestion that traditional Chinese linguistic structures did not capture the cognitive implications of entified Indo-European forms, since it is surely for this reason that the new Chinese forms are evolving.[19]

In the Kung-sun Lung-tzu, a Fourth Century B.C. Chinese philosophical work, discussion focuses centrally on the distinction between property and entified property (e.g., white vs. whiteness; horse vs. horseness), in spite of the linguistic obstacles in its path. But as Wing-tsit Chan (1963) observes in his introduction to selections from the Kung-sun Lung-tzu:

> The school of logicians which produced the Kung-sun Lung-tzu was . . . (of all major ancient Chinese philosophical schools) . . . the only school that was primarily devoted to logical considerations . . . one of the smallest schools . . . (and, moreover, one which) . . . exercised no influence whatsoever after their own time [p. 232].

In other words, what seems most remarkable in this regard is not the appearance of discussion of this distinction in the work of a Chinese philosophical school, but rather its virtual absence from the subsequent tradition of Chinese philosophy despite the fact that it played a central role in an important classical work.[20]

Entification of Conditions and Events

---

[19]See Weinreich, 1968.

[20]For further discussion of this point, see Fung (1952), Needham (1956), 201-202, Hu Shih (1963), and the conclusion to the present chapter.

Moreover the English psycholinguistic processes of entification do not apply only to properties and actions, but to entire conditions and events as well; and it is in application to these latter, more complex structures that the processes of entification seem to make their most dramatic and unique contributions to the shaping of thought.

When, by adjoining nominalizing suffixes and concurrently making use of a nominalizing word-order transformation, the English speaker shifts from "His attitude is sincere" to the "Sincerity of his attitude," from "This rock is hard" to the "Hardness of this rock," from "It is important to be earnest" to the "Importance of being earnest," and from "China has been persistently reluctant to invade Swat" to "China's persistent reluctance to invade Swat," he is not only converting a completed sentence into a noun phrase, but, at the same time, on a cognitive level, moving from the description of a condition that is the case, may be the case, or is not the case, to an extraction of the idea of the condition as a purely theoretical entity. The speaker can go on to state that "The sincerity of Jill's attitude is beyond question" just as easily as he can go on to state that "The sincerity of Jill's attitude is to be seriously questioned" for the mere utterance of the nominalized expression "The sincerity of Jill's attitude" does not commit him to any condition that is or is not the case, but only to the idea of the condition, the notion of it, extracted from the world of actual, imaginary, or potential happenings.

Similarly, in discussing events rather than conditions, when the English speaker shifts from "Interest rates rose" to "The rise of interest rates," and from "That measure will be approved by Congress" to "The approval of that measure by Congress," he not only converts a completed sentence into a noun phrase, but on a semantic level moves from the description of an event that has happened, is happening or will happen to an extraction of the idea of the event as a purely theoretical notion. Starting a sentence with "The approval of this measure by Congress . . . " the speaker can just as easily go on to complete the thought by saying, "The approval of this measure by Congress was faster than expected"—implying that the approval has already occurred—as by saying, "The approval of this measure by Congress will depend on the subcommittee's report"—implying that approval may or may not occur in the future, for "The approval of this measure by Congress . . . " acts only as a signal to transform the event described into a notion in preparation for further processing, rather than as a signal to accept the event as fact.

The English language then, through the structures it affords its speakers, facilitates movement both in speech and in thought, not only from "The kangaroo over there" to the generic kangaroo, from "white" to "whiteness" and from "accept" to "acceptance," but also from "His attitude is sincere" to "The sincerity of his attitude" and from "Interests rates rose" to "The rise of interest rates"—from descriptions of conditions and events to the projection of those conditions and events as theoretical notions, free of truth commitments in the actual world. And a comparison with the Chinese language again reveals that just as that language has not provided its speakers, at least until recent date, with the specific structural means and thus the motivation to create generic entities, or to entify properties or entify actions, neither has it provided them with the specific structural means and thus the motivation to entify conditions and events into truth-commitment-free ideas.

As in the case of the counterfactual, there are various ways by which speakers of Chinese can capture in traditionally Chinese forms roughly the same ideas as those carried by English entified forms. Rather than say "If Bier had been able to speak Chinese, he would have done X, Y, and Z, the Chinese speaker can always make use of the straightforward descriptive statement, "Bier couldn't speak Chinese and therefore he did not do X, Y, and Z." Rather than talk about "Mary's sincerity," the Chinese speaker can always say that "Mary is sincere." Rather than state that "Mary's sincerity cannot be doubted," he can state that "Mary is so sincere, (you) cannot doubt (her)." Rather than say, "Sincerity is a virtue," he can say, "Sincere (i.e., being sincere or acting sincerely, since adjectives in this case are inseparable from verbs) is a virtue." The notion, "John's discovery of that restaurant makes me happy" can be translated into the statement, "John discovered that restaurant, makes me happy." and the statement, "The acceptance of that measure depends on the approval of the subcommittee's report" into the statement "Whether or not that measure is accepted depends on whether or not the subcommittee's report is approved." But these substitute forms, though closely approximating the content of the corresponding English expressions, do not carry the same cognitive implications. Talking of Mary being sincere, of acting sincerely, of John discovering a restaurant, of a measure being accepted or not being accepted, of a report being approved or not being approved, involves talking in terms of a model of the world in which things (or people) have characteristics, and in which things (or people) act, rather than in terms of a model of the world in which these characteristics and happenings have been explicitly transformed into things in themselves, have gained a degree of ontological status independent of the things or people who possess them or the actors who perform them.[21]

Just as contact with Western languages has brought about changes in modern Chinese with respect to the entification of properties, so has it

---

[21]In fact, the independent ontological status of entifications of events is so complete in English that they can be quantified just as any ordinary object—one naturally speaks of "rises of interest rates," "declines in SAT scores," or "frequent discoveries of new bacteria . . . " etc. (I am indebted for this observation to Hugh Lacey).

brought about changes with respect to the entification of conditions and events. Modern Chinese uses what is called the "de" construction (ti) to express equivalents of the English possessive and the English descriptive subordinate clause. The noun to be modified is placed after the particle "de" and the name of the possessor or the subordinated descriptive clause which modifies that noun is placed before the "de." For example, the English phrase "John's book" would translate as "John 'de' book"; the sentence, "The man I met on the street yesterday is the manager of Taipei's largest bank" as "I yesterday met on the street 'de' man is Taipei largest bank 'de' manager"; and the sentence, "Congress just passed a law which imposes a tax on private cars and encourages the use of public transportation" as "Congress just passed an impose tax on private cars and encourage (people) use public transportation 'de' law." The very fact that, in contrast to English, Chinese descriptive clauses precede rather than follow the nouns they modify, itself gives rise to some interesting psycholinguistic consequences. As a result of such "left embedding," the Chinese hearer/reader, by contrast to his English counterpart, must hold in memory the content of the descriptive clause before he/she gains knowledge of what it is that is being described—must code a description, in other words, before constructing the mental representation to which to subordinate that description; and this processing burden seems in turn to place severe constraints on how complex subordinated descriptive clauses can become. The constraints do not relate to length, per se, but rather to the number of internal levels of subordination that a clause can incorporate. One can, for example, freely talk about an "impose tax on private cars, encourage people to use public transportation, discourage the use of gasoline and, at the same time, promote coal, etc., etc., 'de' law, but as soon as a speaker attempts to introduce an additional layer of subordination, for example, by further modifying the term "private cars" with the restrictive clause "used in large cities" to talk about "a law which imposes a tax on the use of private cars in large cities and encourages . . . " (in Chinese—"an impose a tax on in large cities use 'de' private cars and encourage . . .'de' law") then the sentence begins to strain the boundaries of acceptability. As more layers of internal subordination are embedded and more "de" 's are employed to express them, the sentence quickly becomes not only utterly objectionable, but extremely difficult to interpret unambiguously. English speakers have no trouble comprehending what, specifically, is to be discussed when they hear the sentence "We will put off to next week discussion of the further implications of the new method for calculating the relationship between the rate of economic development and individual standard of living." But the direct Chinese translation equivalent, which, by the use of multiple "de" constructions, leaves the levels of internal subordination of the English sentence intact—"We will put off discussing until next week calculate economic development "de" rate and individual standard of living "de" relationship "de" new method "de" further implications"—not only direly offends the aesthetic sensitivities of Chinese speakers, but left 58% (70 out of 120) of the Taiwanese subjects queried unsure as to what exactly will be discussed—further implications, and/or a new method and/or a relationship between economic development and individual standard of living and/or all three, etc. Fluent Chinese might present the relationship first, then in a second sentence talk of the new method of calculating it, and then in perhaps a third sentence state that next week we will talk specifically about the further implications of that method.

Interest in the "de" construction in this context is only indirectly related, however, to the highly interesting limitations it appears to impose in spoken Chinese on the compact expression of internally subordinated speech/thoughts. The principal reason for introducing it stems from the fact that it is the "de" construction which in response to pressures from Western languages has more recently been conscripted by the Chinese language, to serve as its means of entifying conditions and events into truth-commitment-free ideas. The core adjective (in its nominalized form if it has acquired one) or the verb of the condition or event is placed after the "de" in the traditional slot of the noun to be modified, and the remaining components of the description of the condition or event are placed before the "de" in the traditional slot of the possessor or the subordinated descriptive clause. Hence in Hong Kong and Taiwan today, one runs across such constructions as "That matter 'de' importance" equivalent to the English, "The importance of that matter"; "That measure 'de' effectiveness" equivalent to the English, "The effectiveness of that measure"; "His 'de' sincere," equivalent to the English "His sincerity"; "His at school 'de' succeed" equivalent to the English "His success at school"; and "Taiwan 'de' develop" equivalent to the English "The development of Taiwan," in contrast to the traditional Chinese, "That matter is important," "That measure is effective," "He is sincere," "He succeeded at school" and "Taiwan is developing or has developed."

These constructions, although in use, are still considered by many Chinese as corruptive influences that should be eliminated from the language altogether; by a majority of the subjects interviewed as aesthetically less attractive alternatives to the traditional non-entified forms; and by just about everyone, whether they oppose them, favor them, or remain indifferent to them, as prime examples of what is called in Chinese "Westernized Chinese speech." Observations of subject use of them, combined with subject reactions to them and subject ratings of sentences employing them, suggest, moreover, that as soon as a speaker goes beyond the relatively small set of widely used entified structures and attempts to coin new ones, acceptability declines; that as soon as a speaker tries to move from entification of events such as "The rise of interest rates"—in which the interest rates are doing the rising—to the entification of events such as "The approval of this measure"—in which the measure itself is not doing the approving—acceptability tends to decline even more sharply; and that as soon as a speaker attempts to embed internally subordinated information into an entified construction or to embed one entified construction into another, he not only quickly violates the boundaries of acceptability but the boundaries of comprehensibility as well. Thus, in Taiwan today, one can get away with talking about "His theft" and "other people's property" but not with "His theft of other people's property (He other people 'de' property 'de' "thieve"). Hearers will listen to "The sincerity of his attitude" and "His attitude towards democracy" but will not tolerate "The sincerity of his attitude towards democracy" (He towards democracy 'de' attitude 'de' sincere). "The rise of interest rates" and "The importance of interest rates" are both acceptable, but not "The importance of the rise of interest rates"; and it is totally impossible to talk sensibly in this form about "The importance of the acceleration of the rise of interest rates" much less about "The contribution of the rise of overall prices to a decline in the importance of the acceleration of the rise of interest rates," etc. In sum then, the case of entification of conditions and events parallels that of entification of properties. Novel linguistic structures have recently emerged in Chinese in response to Western pressure in order to close a translation gap between Chinese and Western languages. A certain number of such structures have gained currency; but their use still remains far from freely productive.

In an effort to gain some insight into the cognitive underpinnings of these linguistic facts, Chinese and American subjects were presented with the following sample transformations in their native languages:[22]

Paul and Priscilla got married ——→ The marriage of Paul and Priscilla
This thing is important ——→ The importance of this thing.

Subjects were then asked to transform, again in their native languages, the following sentences according to the principle exemplified in the above examples:

A. It is possible that he already arrived ————→
B. Jeremy succeeded ————→
C. His attitude towards that issue is sincere ————→

As one might expect, English-speaking subjects exhibited little difficulty

---

[22]See Appendix for Chinese version.

in extracting the principle exemplified, and in generalizing it across the three sentences presented—in transforming "It is possible that he already arrived" into "The possibility that he already arrived," "Jeremy succeeded" into "Jeremy's success" or "The success of Jeremy" and "His attitude is sincere towards that issue" to "The sincerity of his attitude towards that issue." One-hundred and one out of 116 or 87% of the subjects tested transformed all three sentences correctly, and 115 out of 116 or 99% got two out of three correct. By contrast, only 34 out of 321 or 11% of the Chinese-speaking subjects consistently and accurately generalized the principle of "entification" across the three novel contexts presented, although 197 out of the 321 or 61% got at least one sentence correct. Certainly continued exposure to and use of entified forms can be expected to lead Chinese speakers to develop "entification schemas" and so, for better or worse, to come to think in these Western ways. But one might interpret these data as suggesting that in the meantime there exists a situation in the English-Chinese cross-linguistic arena which closely resembles one often observed in first-language learning, in second-language learning, or even in the mastering of a new discipline. The child or the student begins to make use of a newly acquired linguistic form before he gains command of its full meaning potential, before he has, as it were, consolidated the cognitive schema required for its freely productive use. Then he is led on the basis of the feedback he receives for his use of that form and his observations of others' use of it to construct a cognitive schema for it of the parameters required. Similarly, we might imagine that at some point a small set of "entificational" constructions were introduced into Chinese in order perhaps to translate specific Western thoughts. Monolingual Chinese speakers more recently have begun to assimilate these forms into their own speech without, however, necessarily developing at first the cognitive underpinnings required for their freely productive use. Then as these speakers continue to make use of the forms and to be exposed to their use, they are gradually led by the linguistic experience itself to develop cognitive schemas of the parameters required, schemas which provide the cognitive bases for free generalization of these forms across novel contexts. The fact that language may in this case provide direction to the development of thought rather than the other way around, should, moreover, not be surprising, for as in the case of the counterfactual, the generic concept and the entification of properties and actions, we are dealing with a cognitive schemas whose development does not merely involve further differentiation of the perceptual world but rather a special kind of abstraction from it—in other words, with the sort of schema that is most likely to be dependent for its development on the directives that language provides.[23]

---

[23]For further discussion of the ideas suggested in this paragraph, see Chapter 2.

Entification and
the Construction and Manipulation
of Theoretical Frameworks

Furthermore, one reason, if not the principal reason, why English speakers entify conditions and events is that by so doing the conditions and events can be transformed into individual conceptual units, which can then be fitted, as individual components, into more general theoretical/explanatory frameworks. Contrast, for example, the typical Chinese sentences "He is so industrious, he will certainly succeed" and "Interest rates decline, makes the housing industry grow more rapidly" with their entified English equivalents "His industriousness insures his success" and "The decline of interest rates accelerates the growth of the housing industry." The Chinese sentences call attention to two conditions or two events and then, in addition, stipulate relationships holding between those conditions or events, so that the hearer or reader comes to consider the individual conditions or events on their own terms as well as the intercondition or interevent relationships that link them to one another. By contrast, the entified English sentences convert the subject/predicate descriptions of conditions or events into individual noun phrases and then insert those noun phrases into single subject/predicate frameworks, thereby in effect subordinating the conditions or events to the relationships that link them to one another. The hearer or reader is no longer led to consider the conditions or events on their own terms, but to consider them only as a function of the role they play in the relationships under discussion. The relationships themselves take on a reality of their own, a law-like quality, which derives from the fact that they are understood, not merely as descriptions of observable or imaginable real-world phenomena, but as examples of a different domain of discourse altogether, as theoretical explanatory frameworks designed to provide a clarifying perspective on the world of actual conditions and events and their interrelationships, while at the same time maintaining a certain cognitive distance from the speaker's or hearer's baseline model of that world.

In English the constructions "The fact that . . . " and simply "That . . . " as in "(The fact) that foreign troops line its borders leads that nation to behave conservatively" act in similar manner to signal to the listener or reader that the information being conveyed in the subordinate clause is not to be coded on its own terms, but rather in terms of its contribution to an explanatory model being projected. And just as Chinese traditionally has had no structures equivalent to the English processes of entification of conditions and events, neither has it had structures equivalent to "The fact that . . . " or "That . . . ." So a typical Chinese formulation of the above sentence would take the general form, "Foreign troops line its borders, makes that nation behave conservatively" in which the focus of attention falls on the description of two discrete facts as well as on their inter-relationship rather than on the fact that one fact is being used to explain the other in a projected theoretical model of explanation.

By embedding entified conditions and events within one another, moreover, English speakers can expand their theoretical, explanatory structures into entities of considerable complexity. Whole series of events or conditions can be woven into single theoretical structures with consequent shifts of focus from the component conditions or events to the roles they play in those projected explanatory frameworks. The sequencing of events in the theoretical structures becomes a function of the perspectives the structures are designed to emphasize, rather than of the logical, causal or temporal order in which the component conditions or events have or would have actually occurred. And this further break with actuality serves to further reinforce the psychological impact of the movement away from the world of actual happenings carried by the underlying processes of entification themselves. An English speaker can, for example, take a series of events like:

1. European imperialism in Asia began to wane.
2. At the same time, American presence in Asia began to grow.
3. The two met in conflict.
4. As the conflict accelerated, Japanese leaders became increasingly concerned over protecting sources of raw materials.
5. This increasing concern contributed significantly to their decision to attack Pearl Harbor.

Then, by entifying these events and embedding the entified units into a theoretical, explanatory structure, the speaker can weave them into whatever sequence best befits the needs of his argument. He can state that:

The uncertainties arising from the accelerating conflict between European imperialism and the growth of American presence in Asia, in increasing concern among Japanese leaders over protecting sources of raw materials, contributed significantly to their decision to attack Pearl Harbor;

or, alternatively, that:

Increasing concern among Japanese leaders for protecting sources of raw materials, brought on by the uncertainties arising from the accelerating conflict between the waning of European imperialism and the growth of American presence in Asia, contributed significantly to their decision to attack Pearl Harbor;

or, alternatively, that:

The decision by Japanese leaders to attack Pearl Harbor was significantly influenced by their increasing concern for protecting sources of raw materials brought about in turn by the uncertainties arising from the accelerating conflict between waning European imperialism and the growth of American presence in Asia.

Chinese speakers often characterize such Western recountings of events as insufferably abstract and as "proceeding in circles," for in Chinese, where each event is expressed individually in subject/predicate form, even in complex recountings of interevent relationships, the individual component events seem to retain their individual identities and as such to force the author to remain more closely tied to the logical, temporal, or causal sequence in which they actually fall. A typical Chinese equivalent of all three of the above highly entified examples of English explanatory, theoretical talk might, for example, take the following much more accessible and straightforward form:

While European imperialism began to wane in Asia, American presence began to grow; these two phenomena met in conflict; as the conflict accelerated, Japanese leaders became increasingly concerned how to protect sources of raw materials; strongly influenced them to decide to attack Pearl Harbor.

Furthermore, from a cognitive point of view, we might imagine that repeated exposure to talk of entified conditions and events and to theoretical accountings constructed out of them would over time tend to lead English speakers to develop cognitive schemas that would enable and in fact predispose them not only to move freely in speech from talking about conditions and events as actual or potential occurrences to talking about them as if they were conceptual units of abstracted, theoretical structures, but to move freely in thought as well, from operating with conditions and events and their interrelationships *qua* actual or potential occurrences to operating with them as a function of the roles they play or might be made to play in abstracted, theoretical structures.

Consider the following paragraph and the questions based upon it:

A recent report on pollution stated: Living in a polluted enviroment can cause lung disease; but living in a polluted, comparatively high altitude location increases the danger and, conversely, living in a polluted, low altitude location decreases it. Oddly enough, however, living in a polluted high altitude location and eating a lot of fatty foods turns out to be just like living in a polluted, low altitude location.

According to the above report, which of the circumstances below would be likely to be the most harmful to your health?

A.   A polluted,   low altitude location   and eating a lot of fatty
                                                     foods.

B. A polluted,   relatively high altitude
                        location
                                        and eating a lot of fatty
                                        foods.

C. A polluted,   relatively high altitude
                        location
                                        and eating very little fat-
                                        ty foods

D. Crazy question[24]

A subject might attempt to solve this task by one of two principal strategies. The subject might proceed by focusing systematically on particular conditions, considering in turn people in polluted environments at varying altitudes who do and do not eat lots of fatty foods, and then inferring from the data presented how great a risk of lung disease each group is likely to incur. People who live in polluted, high altitude environments have a greater risk of getting lung disease, while people who live in polluted, low altitude environments have a lesser risk of getting such a disease. But those living in high altitude environments who, in addition, eat lots of fatty foods incur a risk similar to those living in low altitude environments, i.e., a lesser risk. So, living in a high polluted environment and eating little fatty food (i.e., alternative C) is the condition most harmful to health.

Or the subject might approach the task in a very different manner. Rather than proceed to imagine in turn a set of potential real world conditions, he/she might attempt to build, on the basis of the data presented, a theoretical model of the relationships involved. The subject might begin, for example, by interpreting "living in a polluted environment" and "getting lung disease" as two entified notions; fit them as such into the abstracted relationship—the relationship between living in a polluted environment and getting lung disease—; endow that relationship with a reality of its own, so that it, rather than its component conditions, can serve as a basis for the next operation; then proceed to interpret "high altitude" as a factor that strengthens the extracted relationship, "low altitude" as a factor that weakens it, and the entified condition, "the eating of lots of fatty foods" as a factor that acts within the model of theoretical relationships being constructed to negate the effects of "high altitude." The effect of "high altitude," in the absence of the negating factor "the eating of lots of fatty foods," is then the most damaging to health.

Now consider this second version of the above task:

A recent report on pollution stated: There exists a relationship between living in a polluted environment and getting lung disease; at comparatively high altitudes the relationship is stronger and at comparatively low altitudes it is weaker. Oddly enough, moreover, at comparatively high altitudes, eating more fatty foods renders the relationship between living in a polluted environment and getting lung disease equivalent to that existing in low altitude locations.

---

[24]See Appendix for the Chinese text.

According to the above report, which of the circumstances below would be likely to be the most harmful to your health?

A. A polluted, low altitude location and eating a lot of fatty foods.

B. A polluted, relatively high altitude location and eating a lot of fatty foods.

C. A polluted, relatively high altitude location and eating very little fatty foods.

D. Crazy question[25]

This second version is identical in content to the one above and is followed by the same response alternatives; but it is written expressly in terms of relationships rather than conditions, so as to be readily interpretable by the subject who approaches the task by attempting to formulate a theoretical model of the relationships involved and yet to be more difficult to interpret for the subject who approaches the task by attempting to enumerate systematically the conditions involved. If, then, Chinese-speaking subjects are unlikely, as a result of their linguistic environment, to have developed schemas specifically suited to transforming conditions and events into the entified component elements of theoretical frameworks and to operating with them as a function of the roles they play in such frameworks, then they should find the second version of the task appreciably more difficult than the first. And if, by contrast, English-speaking subjects are, as a result of their own particular linguistic environment, likely to have developed schemas specifically suited to transforming conditions and events into the entified component elements of theoretical frameworks and to operating with them as a function of the roles they play in such frameworks, then they (1) should not find the second version of the task appreciably more difficult than the first; (2) should do about as well on the first version of the task as Chinese-speaking subjects of equivalent experience, education and intelligence; but (3) should outperform their Chinese-speaking counterparts on the second version of the task.

Distinct groups of 59 students from Taiwan National University and Hong Kong University (the finest universities in Taiwan and Hong Kong respectively) and 48 students from Swarthmore College responded in their native language to each version of the task—a comparative sample that should offer roughly equivalent levels of experience, education, and intelligence. As summarized in Table 2, the results strongly conform each of the above expectations:

---

[25]See Appendix for Chinese text.

TABLE 2

| | Correct Responses | |
	Chinese Speakers	English Speakers
Version 1	46/59 or 79%	39/48 or 81%
Version 2	31/59 or 59%	38/48 or 79%

Chinese responses to the first version of the task are significantly more accurate than responses to the second version ($X^2{}_{df=1} = 8.41, p < .01$); while English responses remain essentially unaffected by movement from Version One to Version Two. The level of accuracy for Chinese and English speakers is roughly equivalent on Version One; yet on Version Two, English speakers significantly outperform their Chinese counterparts ($X^2{}_{df=1} = 8.19, p < .01$).

The English text of a third, considerably more complex version of the task follows—see appendix for the Chinese text:

John Donahue has the following peculiar characteristics: When the humidity in the atmosphere is relatively low, the hotter the temperature and the less fish he eats, the more comfortable he feels. However, when the humidity is very high, these relationships reverse.

According to the paragraph above, which two of the following conditions make John Donahue least comfortable:

1. high temperature doesn't eat much fish relatively low humidity
2. high temperature doesn't eat much fish very high humidity
3. high temperature eats a lot of fish relatively low humidity
4. high temperature eats a lot of fish very high humidity
5. low temperature eats a lot of fish relatively low humidity

This version differs from the first two in several respects: (1) The correct solution requires the choice of two rather than a single alternative; (2) the paragraph centers on two simultaneous relationships (temperature to comfort; and eating fish to comfort), which are affected by one additional variable (humidity) rather than on one relationship (living in a polluted environment to lung disease), which is affected by two additional variables (altitude and eating fatty foods); and (3) and most significantly, because of the way the paragraph is expressed, there is no way to arrive at an accurate solution to this version of the task unless one attempts to deal with it by constructing a theoretical model of the data presented. The final line of the paragraph instructs the subject to reverse a set of relationships that are not labeled as relationships in the preceding text. If then the subject does not spontaneously project a theoretical model that casts the data as a set of relationships, affected by the additional variable "humidity," he/she has no way to figure out what relationships are to be reversed and hence cannot arrive at an accurate solution. If, however, in reaction to the sentence "The hotter the temperature and the less fish he eats, the more comfortable he feels," the subject turns away from the attempt to imagine John Donahue in a set of distinct situations and projects instead a model of the data in which, under low humidity, hotter temperatures and less fish are each linked in a theoretical relationship to more comfort, then it is easy for the subject to understand that a reversal of these relationships for high humidity would imply that there, low temperature and more fish entail greater comfort—making John most uncomfortable, under low humidity, when the temperature is low and he eats a lot of fish and, under high humidity, when the temperature is high and he eats less fish (i.e., choices #2 and #5.)

Only eight out of 109 or 3% of the Chinese university subjects who responded to this question constructed the theoretical model necessary to arrive at both correct alternatives, as compared to 33 out of 94 or 35% of English-speaking Swarthmore College subjects ($X^2_{df=1} = 24.11, p < .0001$). In later interviewing, Chinese subjects consistently reacted that the question was overly complex, overly abstract and blatantly "unChinese." When I attempted to explain what was required, they responded in effect that they are used to talking and thinking about relationships between people, situations or occurrences, but not about relationships between such things as "eating more fish" and "feeling more comfortable;" in other words, that they are used to talking and thinking about relationships between things that exist or take place within their baseline models of reality but not about relationships between entified things, between reified theoretical entities that have been extracted from those baseline models. English-speaking subjects also found the question very complex and often ambiguous, but they did not perceive it as foreign to their way of speaking and thinking about the world.

When one considers then the English processes of entification—of properties, actions, conditions, and events—and the theoretical accountings to which these processes lead, alongside the generic use of "the" and the English signals of entry into the counterfactual realm, one begins to get a clearer picture of the range of incentives the English language offers for developing cognitive schemas that enable and incline its speakers to shift not only in speech but also in thought from involvement with the world of actual or imagined things, actions, properties, events, or conditions, to the assumption of a detached theoretical perspective on that world—incentives that at least until recent date, have had few if any analogues in Chinese.

Even the English lexical term "theoretical" leads the thoughts of English speakers in directions quite distinct from those to which its Chinese counterpart (lilunshang) points. The Chinese term literally means within or from the perspective of a theory or theory in general. It is currently used in Taiwan to talk about the contents of a specific theory, to contrast what a given theory says with what is actually the case and, by extension, to characterize any argument that smacks of a theory in being abstract, difficult to conceive, complex. "Theoretically speaking" means speaking from the perspective of a given theory or the world of theory. A "theoretical example" is an example of fact taken from the actual world to prove a theory; and the notion "theoretical possibility," to my informants, made no sense at all. But when English speakers say that they are speaking "theoretically," they do not necessarily mean that they are speaking in terms of any given theory or theories, nor that they are necessarily speaking complexly, but rather that they are shifting from description of actual events or even from a description of a given explanation of events incorporated in a given theory to speak as if such were the case, to speak of a consciously hypothesized possible world. For English speakers "a theoretical example" is not a fact taken from the actual world that demonstrates a theory, but a hypothesized example that fits the constraints of a theoretical world being projected. "A theoretical possibility" is one that could occur within the constraints of that projected world. What differentiates the Chinese term for "theoretical" from its English counterpart, then, is that the meaning of the Chinese term derives principally from its link to the noun "theory"; while the English term, although related to the noun "theory" derives its meaning principally from its link to a separate schema that places emphasis, not on the existing set of abstract explanations of phenomena or extensions of that set, but rather on the deliberate severing of truth commitments to the actual world the formulation and projection of theories presuppose. For the Chinese speaker, "speaking and thinking 'theoretically' " remain pretty much confined to the domain of the scientist but, for the English speaker, since they are not equivalent to theory-building, they can become a part of the speaker's everyday linguistic and cognitive activity.

One-hundred fifty-nine Taiwanese subjects, 68 Hong Kong subjects and 112 American subjects of varied backgrounds, age and occupation responded to the following question in their native language:

Everyone has his or her own method for teaching children to respect morality. Some people punish the child for immoral behavior, thereby leading him to fear the consequences of such behavior. Others reward the child for moral behavior, thereby leading him to want to behave morally. Even though both of these methods lead the child to respect morality, the first method can lead to some negative psychological consequences—it may lower the child's self-esteem.

According to the above paragraph, what do the two methods have in common? Please select only one answer.

A. Both methods are useless.
B. They have nothing in common, because the first leads to negative psychological consequences.
C. Both can reach the goal of leading the child to respect morality.
D. It is better to use the second.
E. None of the above answers makes sense (If you choose this answer, please explain).

109 or 97% of the American subjects chose alternative C, for that is in fact exactly what the paragraph says, but only 88 or 55% of the Taiwanese subjects and only 44 or 65% of the Hong Kong subjects made that choice. (The Chinese-English differences are significant at $p < .0001$ ($X^2_{df=1} = 58.32$) and $p < .0001$ ($X^2_{df=1} = 35.30$) respectively). Most of the remaining Chinese-speaking subjects chose D or E and then went on to explain, based on their own experience and often at great length and evidently after much reflection, why, for instance, the second method might be better, or why neither method works, or why both methods have to be used in conjunction with each other, or, perhaps, why some other specified means is preferable. For the majority of these subjects, as was evident from later interviewing, it was not that they did not see the paragraph as stating that both methods lead the child to respect morality, but they felt that choosing that alternative and leaving it at that would be misleading since in their experience that response was untrue. As they saw it, what was expected, desired, must be at a minimum an answer reflecting their personal considered opinion, if not, a more elaborated explanation of their own experiences relevant to the matter at hand. Why else would anyone ask the question? American subjects, by contrast, readily accepted the question as a purely "theoretical" exercise to be responded to according to the assumptions of the world it creates rather than in terms of their own experiences with the actual world. Not a single American subject made reference to his or her own experience. The few American subjects who were unsure about alternative C were concerned with such logical issues as whether "both methods lead . . . " as stated, entails "that each method leads individually . . . " But no American subject appeared to have any difficulty, either of a cognitive or ethical nature, in leaving the actual world aside to work within the constraints of the theoretical world provided, no matter how simplistic or even inaccurate they might hold the content of that world to be.[26]

The contrasting cognitive proclivities of English and Chinese speakers reflected in these data are, moreover, certainly not limited in their influence to the domain of cognitive tasks. The scientific and more broadly philosphical thought of any culture derives ultimately from the cognitive ac-

---

[26]For parallel results among different populations, see Luria, 1976, and Scribner, 1977.

tivities of its individual participants and must, therefore, reflect proclivities inherent in that activity. And the present case is certainly no exception. Needham (1956) in his major work on the history of science in China, presents an impressive array of evidence in support of the claim that traditional China developed both a very rich tradition of empirical observation and an active skeptical orientation, but did not develop a scientific tradition as we know it, for it lacked the third necessary ingredient to such a tradition—namely a theoretical orientation, an inclination to leave the world of practical application behind in an effort to construct and test purely theoretical explanatory frameworks. A disinclination towards the theoretical in this context should not be understood as implying a disinclination towards framing explanations of reality in terms of highly abstract notions, such as "yin," "yang," "li," and "ch'i," but rather as involving a disinclination towards entertaining such abstract notions as truth committment-free hypotheses that retain purely theoreticals status until confirmed by empirical evidence. According to Needham, the one area of mathematics that was least developed in China before the arrival of Western influence was geometry—the area Needham views as most particularly dependent on theoretical rather than practical thoughts. Upon hearing about the research reported in this chapter, a professor of Physics at Swarthmore wondered "whether Chinese mathematics ever developed imaginary numbers, for imaginary numbers much more than negative numbers or even variables, would seem to reflect counterfactual/theoretical thoughts?" Needham (1959) observes that, despite the fact that Chinese mathematics had developed both negative numbers and variables at a very early date, imaginary numbers did not enter Chinese mathematical thought until their introduction from the West; and he then sums up the state of mathematics in traditional China with the following comment: "In the flight from practice into the realm of the pure intellect, Chinese mathematics did not participate" (p. 151).

Joseph Levenson, in *Confucian China and its Modern Fate* (1965), argues that the orientation of even the most empirical branch of Ch'ing Confucianism should be compared to the pre-scientific nominalism of Abelard rather than the inductive science of Bacon. According to Levenson, Bacon and the scientific orientation he spawned, unlike Abelard or the empiricists of the Ch'ing:

> . . . went beyond simply ascribing ultimate reality to the world of phenomena instead of to a hypothetical realm of pure Being. He meant not merely to define the real world but to encroach upon it. It was not enough for him to banish abstractions, which can only be contemplated, in favor of tangibles, which can be observed, for observation was not enough. One had to observe with a method and purpose. Bacon's method was induction from experimentally verified 'irreducible and stubborn facts,' his purpose the eliciting of

general laws for the organization of facts into science . . . [Although according to Levenson the Ch'ing empiricists] . . . might pride themselves . . . on looking around them and 'testing books with facts,' they rarely asked questions systematically which might make them see the essential relevance of some orders of facts to others, they never aspired, as Bacon did, 'to establish forever a true and legitimate union between the experimental and rational faculty.' Though he might go as far as the Renaissance scientist in deprecating search for the universal, eternal form of particular things, the empirically-minded Ch'ing Confucianist had a temper predominantly nominalist, unembarrassing to scientific spirit, but by no means its equivalent nor its guaranteed precursor [Part I, pp. 8-9].

Neither formal logic, nor religious philosophy, nor moral philosophy, nor political philosophy, nor economics, nor sociology, nor psychology, as theoretical systems independent of each other, bearing their own internal systemic constraints and entailments, divorced from the factual content they seek to explain, emerged in China other than as a consequence of importation from the West.[27] The theoretical component of Buddhism tended to be discarded as that religion was assimilated by the Chinese. Confucianism and Taoism both reject the theoretical system-building characteristics of Western religions; the former, in favor of providing precepts for ethical and social conduct, the latter in favor of providing a path by which the individual might bring himself into harmony with the rhythm of nature, rather than distance himself intellectually from it. Maoism, in response to Marx, stresses the integration of theory with practice.

Needham (1956) likewise suggests, however, that Western proclivity for theoretical modeling, while prerequisite to certain stages of scientific advance, was inhibitive to others. Such modeling, he argues, involves the extraction of single patterns of causal explanation from factual data that are in reality characterized by a multiplicity of internal interassociations and interrelationships and hence necessarily gives rise to overly simplistic and constrictive assumptions about the nature of the phenomena it seeks to describe. As Needham sees it, for Western science to have moved beyond classical mechanics to the notion of relativity, it had, in fact, to overcome the narrowing influence of its own purely theoretical perspective; and that was possible only as a result of its confrontation with Chinese philosophical awareness of the infinite interdependence and interrelatedness of natural phenomena, first transmitted to the West, according to Needham, in the work of Liebnitz.

And as the Chinese are quick to observe, it is not only in the realm of science that theoretical thoughts have their inherent shortcomings. In

---

[27]For discussion of a typical early Chinese intellectual response to imported Western scientific ideas, see Sivin, 1970.

choosing to view the world through one theoretical perspective rather than another, to adopt an exclusively political, social, psychological, behavioral, or cognitive view, one easily forgets that one has adopted that perspective for the sake of analysis only and begins to perceive the world and our knowledge of it as inherently compartmentalized in those ways. When analyzing theoretically, moreover, as the Chinese see it, it is particularly easy to separate what is seen as morally right from what is seen as economically, politically, or socially effective; particularly easy to allow a set of abstract justifications and considerations to obscure the concrete effects that a decision or policy may have on individual human beings; and particularly easy to rearrange (i.e., rationalize) one's interpretation of those effects, just as one rearranges events or conditions once entified to fit the needs of a theoretical structure being created. When one projects an abstract, theoretical structure as the explanatory and justifying framework for social or political action—e.g., "saving the world for democracy" or upholding the right of diplomatic immunity—it is particularly easy to allow that structure to take on a moral imperative quality of its own, making it much more difficult to remain flexible to the need for a continuing reexamination of its appropriateness to the changing situation at hand and a continuing reassessment of the moral weight it should carry amongst the conflicting claims involved.[28] And more generally, in moving away from involvement with the real world to the assumption of a theoretical perspective on it, it is particularly easy to delegitimate the dictates of one's own emotional and intuitive life and thereby to undercut the source of one's own sense of personal confidence and autonomy and restrict unnaturally the potential dimensions of one's own experience. From the Chinese point of view, then, the kind of thinking that leads one to accept, if only for the sake of argument, that a triangle is a circle, or that two given methods of moral training are effective even when you known they are not, is a kind of thinking that can often lead not only to an overly simplistic, but also to an alientating, a personally debilitating, and, in fact, an amoral perspective on the world.[29]

---

[28]See Kelman, 1973 and Sanford and Comstock, 1971.

[29]Within Kohlberg's theory of moral development (see Kohlberg 1969, 1971; Lickona, 1976) a theoretical approach to morality, or more specifically the construction of a personal, theoretical moral framework based on consciously derived and deliberately formalized universal principles, is seen as prerequisite to the attainment of the highest stage of moral thought. Hence it is not surprising that Kohlberg found so few subjects in his Chinese sample who he interprets as having reached that stage. One can, however, ask whether the core of that stage should be considered the construction of such a formalized theoretical value framework, or whether it should be seen rather as the development of an autonomous moral orientation that may or may not take such a formalized form. Under this latter assumption, movement from a feeling of responsibility to accept unanalytically the demands of the state and/or society to a feeling of responsibility to become one's own moral arbiter, to weigh and resolve personally

F.S.C. Northrop (1946) in *Meeting of East and West* contrasts the Orient's propensity for analyzing things with respect to their perceptual, aesthetic component with the Occident's propensity for analyzing things with respect to their theoretic component. André Malraux (1961) in *Temptation of the West*, writes from the perspective of a young Chinese who is reacting to the impact of Western thought on his society:

But we *experience* this existence: it dominates and shapes us without our being able to grasp it. We are filled with it, since we are men, while you are geometers, even of divinity . . . [p. 22] . . . Confronted with a chaotic universe, what is the first requirement of the mind? To comprehend the universe. But we are unable to do this with the images it offers us, since we immediately realize how transitory they are; thus we try to assimilate its rhythm. Experiencing the universe is not the same as systematizing it, no more than experiencing love is the same as analyzing it. Only an intense awareness achieves understanding. Our thinking . . . is not as is yours, the result of a body of knowledge, but it is the equipment, the preparation for knowledge. You analyze what you have already felt; we think in order to feel [p. 87].

Marcel Granet (1934) observes in *La pensée chinois*:

Themes evocative of free meditation, that is, what the Chinese demand of their Sages, and not ideas—no less dogmas . . . The Chinese have no taste for abstract symbols. They see within Time and Space only a collection of occasions and locations. It is the interdependencies, the solidarities which constitute the order of the Universe. The Chinese doesn't believe that man can form a reign in nature or that the mind can disengage itself from the material . . . Law, the abstract, and the unconditional are excluded—the Universe is one—as much with respect to its societal as with respect to its natural aspect . . . Hence the despise of all that involves uniformity, of all that would permit induction, deduction or any form of constraining reasoning or calculation . . . [pp. 473-79, translation mine].

And the Third Century B.C. Confucian philosopher, Hsun-tzu, in reacting to the work of the Kung-sun Lung-tzu, makes the following comment (Needham, 1956):

There is no reason why problems of "hardness and whiteness," "likeness and

---

the moral claims present in any given conflict situation, would become the mark of post-conventional reasoning, and the resolution of such claims based on considered intuition would count as highly as an approach based on logical deduction from a formalized theory of right and wrong, as long as in each case the resolution is autonomously performed. Confucius, Mencius, and Lao-tzu as well as Aristotle, Montaigne, and Camus would then be admitted along with Plato and Rawls into the pantheon of higher stage post-conventional thinkers, and the post-conventional thinkers in Chinese samples would emerge classified as such, as they did in a questionnaire survey relating to this point conducted in Hong Kong in 1973 (see Bloom, 1977a; 1977b).

unlikeness,'' "thickness or no thickness'' should not be investigated, but the superior man does not discuss them; he stops at the limit of profitable discourse [p. 202]. [The use of '-ness' is a function of translation]

Historically-speaking, it is certainly not the case that structural differences between Chinese and English bear primary responsibility for creating the culturally-specific modes of thinking reflected in the above quotations and in the findings of this chapter as a whole. From a historical point of view, languages are much more the products of their cultures than determiners of them. What one can and cannot express distinctly in any particular language at any particular point in its development is the aggregate result of the totality of social, political, environmental, and intellectual influences that have, from generation to generation, affected its speakers' lives. A new insight, a new experience, a new discovery, a new invention, a new institution, or new contacts with another language-world lead to the development of new linguistic forms. The disappearance of old ways of thinking, of out-worn conventions, and of objects, which have no use in the present scene, lead to the disappearance of the linguistic forms that had been used to speak about them. Historically-speaking, the fact that Chinese has not offered its speakers incentives for thinking about the world in counterfactual and entificational ways is likely to have contributed substantially to sustaining an intellectual climate in which these modes of thinking were less likely to arise;[30] but if Chinese speakers at some point in the past had felt a sufficient need to venture into the realm of the counterfactual or the theoretical, the Chinese language would have evolved to accommodate that need, as it is doing today. And so, to explain historically why counterfactual and entificational thinking did not develop on a general scale, one would have to look not only to the characteristics of the language but to the social and intellectual determinants of why a perceived need for such thinking did not arise. Similarly, the proliferation of new Western modes of speech in present-day Hong Kong and Taiwan society is certainly contributing significantly to the proliferation in turn of Westernized modes of thought, but to understand why more recently Chinese speakers have began to construct forms to match those of Western languages, and to explain why, once these forms emerge, they are assimilated rather than rejected, as they may very well have been in the past—on the grounds that they lead speakers "beyond the limit of profitable discourse''—one has to look beyond the characteristics of the language to the social, political, and intellectual pressures that have in effect guided the language's development during the past fifty years.

But the argument of this book is not about the role languages play in shaping their own historical development—in contributing to the creation

---

[30]See Hu Shih, 1963.

or maintenance of intellectual climates in which specific linguistic forms are more or less likely to emerge. Nor is it about, in more general terms, how languages come to have the specific forms that they have; but it is rather about how languages, through the forms they do and do not have, lead their speakers within each generation to come to be participants in and bearers of distinctive cognitive worlds. It is not about why the Chinese language did not traditionally develop forms for counterfactual and entificational ways of speech or why Western languages did, but rather about the effects such linguistic facts have within each generation on their speakers' cognitive lives.

2

Linguistic Initiatives in the Shaping and Functioning of Thought

This chapter turns from the investigation into the distinctive impacts of the Chinese and English languages on their speakers' thoughts to an examination of the psychological mechanisms through which those distinctive impacts might be seen to take place, with the aim of supplying a supportive theoretical framework for the interpretations advanced in Chapter 1 and of providing a clearer picture of the nature of the contributions languages make to their speakers' cognitive lives.[1]

Let us start from the epistemological view shared by the Cognitive Structuralists[2] that we impose meaningful organization on the infinitely varying world of sense experience, by means of a highly complex and extensive repertory of discrete cognitive schemas. According to this view, our schemas permit us to divide up and conquer the world cognitively-speaking, to segment it cognitively into the types of objects, actions, relations, and properties we perceive to exist in it; to recognize the particular instances we encounter as examples of the types of objects, actions, relations, and properties with which we are familiar, and to store information gained from our experiences with particular instances in a way so that that information can be readily applied in our future interactions with instances of the same kind. These schemas serve as well as the cognitive building blocks of the representations we construct of the situations we encounter, of the action alter-

---

[1]For recent summaries of experimental investigations into the impact of language on thinking at the individual psychological level, see Clark and Clark, 1977, 554-557; Cole and Scribner, 1974, 39-60; Foss and Hakes, 1978, 384-394; Oléron, 1977,67-115; and Slobin, 1979, 143-185. See also Piaget, 1926, and Cole, Gay, Glick, and Sharp, 1971.

[2]See, among others, Piaget, 1960, 1971; Piaget and Inhelder, 1969; Fodor, 1975.

natives we see as available in those situations, and of the probable consequences of these action alternatives, on the basis of which we decide what
we will do. They constitute the component elements of the thoughts we
think and the nodes around which we construct our more permanent, long-
term models of the world. And if language is to influence our cognitive life,
according to this view, then it must do so either by influencing the development of, or by influencing the functioning of, these schematic building
blocks of that life. If, in other words, we adopt a view of human cognition
based on the metaphor of a complex array of discrete cognitive schemas,
then the Whorfian question—the question of if and how the language/s we
learn might influence the way we think—seems to reduce to two, empiri-
cally-speaking, more readily approachable subquestions: (1) How, if at all,
might the languages we learn influence the development of the parameters
of the cognitive schemas in which we come to think? and (2) How, if at all,
might the languages we learn come to influence the functioning of those
cognitive schemas once they are formed?

LANGUAGE AND THE SHAPING
OF OUR COGNITIVE REPERTORIES

In an attempt to deal with the first subquestion, let us take a look at how a
child might proceed to impose schematic organization on his or her world,
focusing our attention on where and how the language/s he or she learns
might affect that process. One might posit along with Piaget that the child
comes into the world with little more determined than a preprogrammed
propensity for actively constructing and refining schemas through the processes of assimilation and accommodation. Or one might posit along with
Chomsky[3] that the child comes into the world equipped with a predetermined
propensity, at least as far as his syntactic competence is concerned, for constructing schemas of certain general kinds, bearing certain specifically
determined constraints. Or one might posit along with Fodor[4] that the child
in fact comes into the world already equipped with an array of specifically
determined, primitive schemas that constitute the building blocks of all further schema construction and differentiation. But however specified the
child's innate structure, there is little question that the child must proceed
on the basis of it to build a far more complex and differentiated cognitive
mapping of the world. He must possess or construct schemas to serve as the
cognitive bases for recognizing the general kinds of objects, actions and
properties that exist within his world, the particular individuals, objects and

---

[3]See, among others, Chomsky, 1965, 1968, and 1975.
[4]See Fodor, 1975.

locations that populate it, and the various types of generic relations that can occur in it (e.g., the relation between an actor and an action, a possessor and a possession, or an object and the location in which it is to be found or to be placed).[5] He must already have or construct schemas roughly equivalent to the English notions "people," "Rover," "talk," "bark," and action/agent, in order to make sense out of what is going on in a situation in which people are talking or Rover is barking, in order to store the general facts that people talk and that Rover barks and even perhaps in order to record the specific memory that Rover barked at that particular moment in time.[6]

Through the construction, differentiation, and integration of such schemas, the normal child will, if Piaget is correct, succeed by around eighteen months in building quite an adequate mapping of the sensations, objects, actions, and relations that surround him—a mapping permitting him not only to recognize and understand the individual instances of his world but to recognize, understand and predict the relations that hold and can hold between them; to recognize, understand and predict how he and other persons and objects move in space, where balls that roll under couches are to be found, how to take the shortest path between two points. He will have, in Piaget's terminology, transcended his formerly egocentric perspective on the sensory-motor world to come to understand that world, for all his intents and purposes, as it is.[7]

If Piaget is likewise correct, however, during the child's first year and a half of schema construction, language will play a very limited role in influencing the way he comes to divide up and conquer the world. During his first eighteen months, exposure to adult speech and reinforcements received for producing, or at least approximating it, are likely to lead the child to construct schemas suited for recognizing and/or articulating some of the particular sounds of the adult language and to construct even more complex schemas suited to recognizing and/or articulating specific sequences of those sounds—i.e., words. The child is likely as well to construct functional or associative links between some of the specific words that he recognizes or articulates and other elements of his cognitive world. He may, for example, develop a facility (i.e., schema) for articulating the word "mommy" and link the use of that schema to a schema denoting "mother's attention," thereby building the cognitive basis for employing that word as a functional means of eliciting that desired state. Or he may link the word "doggie" (or more precisely the schema through which he recognizes and/or articulates it) to his pet teddy bear (or more precisely the schema through which he

---

[5]See Brown, 1973.
[6]See Tulving's, 1972, distinction between semantic and episodic memory.
[7]See Piaget, 1952.

codes its existence) and hence begin to make use of the word "doggie" in association with his interactions with his pet teddy bear. But throughout his first year and a half of life, the words that the child learns will, according to Piaget, constitute mere additional elements of his cognitive world, on a par with other elements, and in some cases linked to them by functional or associative bonds. They will not yet be understood or used as symbols that can stand in the place of other elements of that world for the purposes of communication or thought. And because words merely constitute elements onto themselves, rather than symbols for other categorizations, they will not yet be capable of exerting the kind of influence over the child's developing schematic mapping of the world that they will later on.

At around eighteen months, however, at the point Piaget marks as the onset of stage six of sensory-motor development, and Vygotsky[8] describes as the moment when thought and speech converge, in the view of these two psychologists, the capacity for symbolization develops and with it the capacity to link one set of schemas to another as signals of, symbols for, that other set. And so the child begins to link "lexical" schemas, such as those through which he already recognizes and/or articulates the sound sequences "mommy," "red," or "crawl," to cognitive schemas, such as those through which he already divides the world into his mother, red things, and acts of crawling, and by so doing, gains mastery for the first time of the use of words as linguistic labels for cognitive divisions of his world. He constructs schemas for recognizing and/or articulating distinct intonational contours, links those "intonational schemas" in turn to schemas in his cognitive repertory through which he recognizes such cognitive acts or states as wanting, questioning, and asserting, and by so doing, gains mastery of the use of intonational contours as linguistic labels for cognitive acts or states.[9] He constructs schemas for recognizing and manipulating distinct word classes (e.g., nouns, noun phrases, verbs, etc.) and for recognizing and manipulating distinct sequences of word classes (e.g., noun phrase + verb + adverb vs. noun phrase + verb + noun phrase), links the distinct sequences of word classes he constructs in turn to cognitive schemas that divide the world into distinct generic relations (e.g., agent/action/manner vs. agent/action/object), and by so doing gains mastery of the use of word class sequences as linguistic labels for the relations he perceives to exist between the actors, objects, and actions of his world.[10] In time, he will construct even more complex "grammatical" schemas for recognizing and manipulating functor words, inflections, and complex sentence paradigms such as the passive, the negative question, the

[8]See Vygotsky, 1962.
[9]See Greenfield and Smith, 1976; Searle, 1969.
[10]See Brown, 1970, 75-154; Brown, 1973; Macnamara, 1972.

tag question, the counterfactual, or the entification of conditions and events—i.e., sentence paradigms that seem to lend themselves to transformational description. He will link these more complex "grammatical schemas" in turn, transformationally or heuristically,[11] to the particular cognitive divisions of the world which, in his language, are appropriate to them, and by so doing, gain mastery of the use of the more complex syntactic signaling devices his specific linguistic system provides.[12]

In brief, the emergence of the ability to symbolize and thus to use words, intonational contours and grammatical structures as signals of particular cognitive perspectives of the world opens the door to linguistic communication. But once equipped with this ability, the child has still to master the words, intonational contours and grammatical structures specific to his language and then to attach them individually to cognitive divisions of the world appropriate to them. And if appropriate cognitive schemas are not available in his repertory, he will have to transform and supplement that repertory, where necessary, so that it comes to include schemas of the parameters required. To learn the language of his adult culture, he will, in other words, have not only to learn words, intonational contours, and grammatical structures, but to reformulate and extend his cognitive map of the world in the directions to which his language points, so that he can come to mean and understand by his use of these linguistic labels what adults of his culture do by theirs.

The child will certainly continue, and in fact continue throughout life, to construct a very large number of cognitive schemas, on his own, free of any influence exerted by the language/s he learns to speak. He will construct schemas for making beds, for typing papers, for recognizing that his car is skidding on a patch of ice, and for storing motor information as to how to deal with it; schemas for recognizing the kinds of subtle tensions present in various types of social interaction and for storing information as to what kinds of gestures, facial expressions and/or changes of intonation might be most effective in defusing them; schemas for recognizing the styles of given authors, painters, or musicians; for finding certain things funny and for being cute or ironic himself; for sizing up differing personalities and monitoring his response to them; for attending to spatial arrangements and color coordinations and for manipulating them; for matching his lecture style to the moods of his audience, his prose style to the formality of the occasion, for appreciating what good style is, and even for "intuitively" weighing moral claims and drawing causal inferences—schemas that will neither be shaped by nor labeled by the language/s he comes to speak—schemas that will remain, in other words, components of his inordinately complex array of non-labeled thoughts.

---

[11]See Bever, 1970.
[12]See Brown, 1970, 155-207 and Ferguson and Slobin, 1973, part 2.

And the child will also continue to construct a great number of schemas for which at a later point in time he will discover, often with some ounce of satisfaction, that labels exist either in his language or in another. He is likely, for instance, to construct a cognitive category corresponding roughly to the English labeled schema "red" even if he has not been exposed to a label that directs them to do so.[13] And he is likely to divide the world cognitively into the generic relations agent/action vs. possessor/possession vs. agent/location, etc., even before he learns the grammatical labels his language uses to express them. So, in these cases, he has only to attach the linguistic labels as he acquires them, to schemas from his cognitive repertory already appropriate to them to become master of their linguistic use.[14] Likewise, there is reason to suppose that a child might divide the world as well into lawns vs. trees, hungry vs. thirsty, color vs. shape, depressed vs. elated, figure out vs. confused, succeed vs. fail, infer vs. explain, and pumpkin vs. grapefruit before he masters the linguistic labels appropriate to these cognitive divisions of the world, for as in the case of "red" or agent/action, or possessor/possession, the parameters of these divisions have a perceptual, functional, or subjective salience of their own.

In addition, however, both to developing a large number of schemas free of the influence of language, which never come to be labeled and to developing a large number of schemas free of the influence of language, which come in time to be labeled, but whose internal organization remain unaffected by the fact that they receive labels, the child will construct or reconstruct a very large number of schemas expressly to meet the requirements of linguistic labels. By contrast to red things or typewriters, dogs, for instance, as a class are not perceptually-speaking especially similar to each other, or especially distinct from neighboring categories of things.[15] Consider how much more a dachshund resembles a squirrel, cat, or beaver, than it does a great Dane. And so it is not surprising that a child is not likely to develop on his own, a schema appropriate to the labeled category "dog." The schema to which the child attaches the label "dog" often embodies too broad a segmentation of reality, leading the child to apply the label "dog" once he acquires it, not only to dogs but to all furry things including horses and blankets;[16] or the schema may be too narrow in scope, leading the child to apply the label, for example, to Rover, his pet, but to Rover alone. If the child is in this case to learn to use the label correctly, he will have to readjust the parameters of the categorization of reality to which it has become attached; he will have to attend to the adult use of the word and to reactions

---

[13]See Rosch, 1973, 1977.
[14]See Brown, 1973.
[15]See Rosch, 1978.
[16]See Clark, 1973.

to his own use of it and on the basis of that information gerrymander appropriately his cognitive mapping of the world. Similarly, to learn to use distinctly and correctly the labels, "magazine," "newspaper," "comic book," "catalogue," "brochure," "journal" and "periodical," or the labels "bachelor," "sister," "first cousin," "diplomatic immunity," "nominalism," or "GNP," the child will have to readjust and/or extend in new directions his cognitive mapping of the world until it comes to include the cognitive divisions these labels require.[17]

Let us, just by way of theoretical example, take the English label "amount" and explore how a child might go about constructing a cognitive schema appropriate to it. The notion "amount" is particularly difficult for it involves entertaining the idea of an abstract entity that manifests itself in perceptually distinct forms. Certainly just supplying the word and pointing simultaneously to a glass of water will not be sufficient to alert the child to the fact that "amount" refers to an abstract aspect of the water, rather than

---

[17]According to Rosch (1978), our cognitive categories are formulated around representations of prototypical instances, such as the prototypical dog, mountain, or machine, against which encountered instances are compared to assess whether they do or do not belong to the category in question. Under such an interpretation, the child can be seen as having to readjust former prototypes or to construct new ones to effect the cognitive divisions of the world that his language requires. According to Clark (1973), Katz and Postal (1964), and Katz (1972) by contrast, our cognitive categories are formulated in terms of integrations of "semantic atoms" (e.g., animate, non-human, furry, four-legged, and barks) or, for Kintsch (1974), in terms of integrations of more complex, internally-structured proposition lists (e.g., Is animate; Is non-human; Is furry; Has four legs; Barks)—in present terminology in terms of integrations of more elementary cognitive schemas—which in combination act as the evaluative criteria by which membership in the category is determined. Under this interpretation, the child can be seen in some cases as having merely to reshuffle more elementary cognitive schemas he already has available into new combinations to create the schemas his language requires, while in other cases as having to await the development of new schemas, of new modes of categorizing experience, which are needed to serve as building blocks to the construction of the more complex categorizations of reality his language demands. One might alternatively imagine that the child's schemas contain both prototype and property list components (i.e., semantic atoms or propositions), since as adults at least we do seem to have access both to prototypes for dogs, men and women, bachelors, theories, and forces and to property lists that stipulate necessary and sufficient conditions for being a dog, man, woman, bachelor, theory, or force, with those categories as a result more specifically defined. Under this latter interpretation, the child can be seen as having to proceed simultaneously to reformulate both prototypes and property lists if he is to equip himself with the cognitive schemas necessary for gaining appropriate use of the labels of his language.

The property list components of cognitive schemas seem, moreover, to be more amenable to conscious readjustment than do the prototype components. Upon hearing a new defining attribute of "electron," which falsifies a feature we held to be true of electrons, we can simply replace the new piece of information for the old in our property list for electron and by so doing come to use the concept "electron" in an adjusted way. However, to readjust a prototype we may have developed, for instance, for "woman" or "Communist" we seem to require a much more long-term change in experience and/or a long term rise in consciousness.

to its perceptual attributes (e.g. its shape, color, or feel) or to its function (i.e., drinkability). And certainly, providing a definition like "An amount is an abstract quantity whose physical manifestations are all equivalent" will not assist the child at this point in his life in the difficult task of appropriate schema construction.

What the child might do to begin the process of mastering the notion "amount" is to attach the label "amount" to a schema in his repertory, which on the basis of his observations of adult use of the word seems most appropriate to it. Let us say that the schema chosen is one relating to the perceptual parameters (i.e., the size) of observed objects. When his mother asks him what "amount" of clay he wants, he points out the physical parameters of the piece he wants. His mother smiles, and he feels relatively confident in his understanding and use of the word. But one morning he is served a tall thin glass of Koolaid and his sister a short fat glass, and he begins to complain about the inequality of treatment. Mother responds, "But, Johnny, you and your sister both have the same amount"; and Johnny, who generally grants credibility to his mother, begins to wonder whether he misunderstands the word "amount," for in fact the perceptual parameters and hence the "amount"—as he understands the word—of Koolaid are different. On another occasion, Johnny finds himself with two quarters while his friend has five dimes, different amounts of money by his criteria; yet surprisingly, both are termed by the candy store owner to be the same "amount" of money and both turn out to be equivalent for the purposes of purchasing candy. These and analogous experiences lead Johnny to rethink his meaning of "amount," not necessarily consciously, of course, and to conclude that "amount" has something to do not only with the physical parameters of substances but also with the fact that they are equivalent with respect to some purpose such as drinking or buying candy— yet equivalence in physical parameters seems to contradict at times equivalence for special purposes, and Johnny is left with a dilemma. Independent experiences may help. Let us say that in attempting to master concepts such as "number," "opinion" or "idea," Johnny gets a notion of what an abstract entity might be by contrast to a perceptually apprehendible one. He can then draw upon that newly mastered schema for "abstract entity" to resolve his dilemma with his developing notion of "amount." By incorporating the notion of abstract entity into his schema for "amount," he can, in other words, come to understand and use the word as referring not to the physical parameters of a substance but to an abstract quantity of that substance whose instances are equivalent with respect to some purpose. Moreover, further experience with instances of liquids labeled the same "amount" may lead Johnny to the further realization that if two instances of water are labeled the same "amount," if one looks taller, the other must be wider—in other words, to the realization on an intuitive level that if two instances of liquid are the same "amount," the product of the dimensions of one must equal the product of the dimensions of the other; and Johnny may then add this further insight to his growing understanding of the notion "amount." Or, his mother may try to demonstrate to Johnny that he and his sister indeed have the same amount of Koolaid by pouring the Koolaid from each of their differently shaped glasses sequentially into a third glass and pointing to the fact that the liquid from each of the original glasses comes up to the same level in the third glass. The demonstration may not only convince Johnny of the justice of the situation, but in addition lead him to discover a valid way to test if two liquids in differently shaped containers are the same amount; and that test may be incorporated as one more criterial property of his increasingly refined schema for "amount."

In this theoretical example, mastery of the word "amount" can certainly not be said to be equivalent to mastering the notion "amount," nor can the word "amount" be said to have created on its own the cognitive schema that came to underlie it. But the word can be said to have acted (1) as a directive force in leading Johnny to think about the world in certain novel ways and (2) as a locus around which the results of that thinking came to coalesce.

Other linguistic labels such as "distinctive feature," "French Revolution," "Marxism," or "pancreas" will call upon Johnny to search for new knowledge while giving direction to and acting as the points of condensation around which the acquisition of that further knowledge proceeds. Still others will call upon him to build new explicit analytic frameworks by drawing on knowledge that he already implicitly has. He is likely to know at a young age that the sentence "If you hold this glass with only one hand you will break it" does not imply that there are no other ways of breaking it, yet that the sentence "If you eat your dinner, you can go to the movies" in context does imply that eating dinner is the only way (See also Chapter 1). So the labels "if-then" and "if-and-only-if-then" when he encounters them in logic class will not motivate him to seek new knowledge, but rather to extract from experience he already has the information necessary for constructing new schemas that enable him to understand and make explicit use of the formal distinction between if-then and if-and-only-if-then relations. The label "analogy" will direct him to think about comparisons he and others have made between objects or events with similar properties or effects, and to extract from those comparisons the explicit analytic perspective the notion "analogy" embodies. And 'analogously' the grammatical label "had. . . would have " will lead Johnny to draw upon his prior experiences with implications and with imagined situations known to be false in the construction of a new schema that represents an achieved integration of the two and that thus provides him with the cognitive basis for adopting an explicitly counterfactual mode of categorizing and operating with the world.

Other labels will lead Johnny to make use of labeled divisions of reality he has already constructed as building blocks to the construction of even more complex labeled divisions. To construct a schema for "bachelor," for example, he will have to make use of already consolidated schemas for "man" and "unmarried"; to construct a schema fully appropriate to the label "court," he will have to make use of a consolidated schema for "law"; to construct a schema appropriate to the label "political science," he will have to make use of schemas for "government," "nation," and "international relations"; and to construct a schema that will provide adequate mastery of the label "Behaviorism," he will have to make use of schemas for, among others, "theory," "behavior," "prediction," "control," "stimulus," "response," "reinforcement," and "operant." Furthermore, the labels of the language he is learning will guide him to further refine and elaborate many of the schematic perspectives on the world he has already developed so that those perspectives come to include as part of their defining parameters the logico-linguistic links they bear to one another in the adult linguistic world. His notion of red will come to include as one of its defining criteria its link to his notion color; his notion mammal will come to include among its defining criteria its links to elephant, weasel, platypus, as well as to "vertebrate" and "nourishes young with milk," Johnny will come to know, in other words, that daisies are flowers, that bachelors are male, and that no triangles have four sides, just as he knows that if two instances of water are the same amount, the product of their dimensions must be equal, not as a function of his direct experience, but rather, analytically, as a function of the internal defining parameters of the cognitive schematic world his linguistic labels have led him to construct.[18]

Johnny will then build on the basis of non-linguistic experience alone, the cognitive underpinnings necessary for mastering the appropriate use of many of the labels of his language, but for many others he will depend on linguistic labels to guide him to the cognitive accomplishments he requires. And the more complex the structured perspective on reality to which a label points, the more extracted that perspective from immediate experience, and the more dependent that perspective, for the definition of its parameters, on the links it bears to other labeled schemas in the linguistic web, the more likely it is that if Johnny is to develop that particular mode of categorizing reality at all, he will have to rely on a linguistic label—lexical, intonational, or grammatical—to point the way and to serve as the locus around which the processes of cognitive construction required for it take place. Think of

---

[18] See Katz, 1944; and Putnam, 1971.

how improbable it would be for a child or an adult to come to construct, on the basis of non-linguistic experience alone, the particular cognitive divisions of the world signaled by such English lexical labels as "amount," "bachelor," "Behaviorism," or "law;" "metonomy," "psycholinguistics," "Existentialism," or "relativity." And think of how improbable it would be for a child or an adult to come to construct the particular cognitive divisions of the world signaled by such English grammatical labels as "if he had gone" by contrast to "if he went," "hardness" by contrast to "hard," and "his contribution to that movement" by contrast "he contributed to that movement"—if linguistic labels were not to intervene to give direction to the process and to serve as the points of condensation around which the appropriate cognitive schemas form.[19]

Linguistic labels, then, by leading the child to reformulate and extend his repertory of cognitive schemas in the specific directions they require, in effect lead the child to equip himself with whatever additional cognitive bases he needs for full participation in the linguistic communication processes of his culture. But the schemas that the child constructs or reconstructs under the guidance of these linguistic labels will not only serve him as the cognitive bases for his communicative acts. They will take their place alongside the schemas he has developed on his own as additional cognitive structures through which he will make sense out of and process information about the world. They will serve him alongside those schemas that he has developed, on his own, free of the influence of language, as supplementary building blocks of the representations he constructs of the situations he encounters, of the action alternatives he sees as available in those situations, and of the probable consequences of those action alternatives. They will serve as supplementary components of the thoughts he will think and as supplementary organizing modes of his long-term memories. We represent the world to think about it, to react to it and to remember things about it in terms of categories we have developed on our own without the assistance of our language; but we also represent the world to think about it, to react to it and to store information about it in terms of such categories as "bachelor," "theory," "diplomacy," "revolution," "inflation," "Behaviorism," and "law"; in terms, in other words, of structures to which we have been led by our linguistic labels.[20]

---

[19]See Blank (1975) for discussion of the role of the word "why" in leading the child to develop the cognitive abilities, which "would otherwise remain undeveloped" (p. 50), that are required for appropriate use of, and response to, that question word—abilities including those of seeking and understanding explanations in terms of such abstract dimensions as motivation (e.g., 'He lay down because he wanted to rest'), condition (e.g., 'He lay down because his back hurt'), causation (e.g., Things sink because . . .) and justification (e.g., I think he was angry because . . .), p. 45.

[20]Fodor (1975) argues that in order to master a concept embodied in a language one must first be able to represent that concept as a hypothesis in a language, natural or cognitive, one

Learning a new discipline largely consists in coming to understand and use appropriately the individual labeled schemas that constitute its fundamental vocabulary. Labeled schemas such as "distribution of wealth" or "Third World" play active roles in the way we categorize the political world and hence in the way we construct our attitudes to it. Lexical schemas like "rhyme," "rhythm," and "metaphor" provide the blueprint for the initial analysis of poems. Labeled schemas like "Renaissance" and "Gang of Four" serve as nodes of memory around which entire knowledge clusters are built. Labeled schemas drawn from computer technology such as "input," "output," "storage," and "address" provide structuring frameworks for investigations in cognitive psychology. Labeled schemas like "sin," "salvation," "excommunication," "transubstantiation," "nirvana," "tao," and "sabbath" lead members of religious communities to develop the shared perspectives on reality they require. Labeled schemas like "Bachelor of Arts," "Ph.D," "judicial appeal," "extradition," "in-

---

already knows. Hence learning a new language, including one's first natural language, cannot increase the expressive power one already has at one's disposal. One must at birth be already equipped with all of the cognitive ingredients necessary for constructing all the concepts one will ever construct. If Fodor is correct in this claim, however, then conceptual development is a function of learning to integrate primitive cognitive ingredients in new, more complex ways; hence what is relevant to present concerns is the role words play in giving direction to certain of these integrations. And in this respect, Fodor argues: (1) that there is not " . . . any need to deny the Whorfian point that the kinds of concepts one has may be profoundly determined by the character of the natural language that one speaks." (p. 85); and (2) that this can be true, for the new integrations to which words lead take their place in the child's representational system—his language of thought—both as supplementary schemas for the processing of information and as supplementary building blocks for further elaborations of the representational system itself:

> But, though it might be admitted that the *initial* computations involved in first language learning cannot themselves be run in the language being learned, it could nevertheless still be claimed that, a foothold in the language once having been gained, the child then proceeds by extrapolating his bootstraps: The fragment of the language first internalized is itself somehow essentially employed to learn the part that's left. This process eventually leads to the construction of a representational system more elaborate than the one the child started with, and this richer system mediates the having of thoughts the child could not otherwise have entertained [p. 83].

Moreover, Fodor presents an array of linguistic evidence in support of the claim that many of the schemas in our internal language of thought are equivalent to labeled concepts of our natural language (pp. 99-156); and, similarly, semantic memory theorists, although not necessarily committed to any side of the Whorfian issue, find it useful to make use of many concepts directly equivalent to those of natural language as the nodes of their theoretical models of long-term memory (see, among others, Collins and Loftus [1975]; Kintsch [1974]; Rumelhart, Lindsay, & Norman [1972]; Smith, Shoben, & Rips [1974]; and Winograd [1977]). If our systems of internal representation contain schemas equivalent to such natural language labels as "bachelor," "pancreas," "France" or "philosophy," it is reasonable to suppose that natural language labels must exert a directive influence over their development.

dividual rights,'' ''tort,'' ''misdemeanor,'' ''felony,'' ''election,'' ''candidate,'' and ''political party'' lead participants in educational, legal, and political systems to come to define legal and political reality in shared ways and hence make possible the very existence of the systems as abstract shared, social entities. And schemas such as those of mood, tense, aspect, presupposition, counterfactuality or entification, to which we are led by grammatical labels, transcend content boundaries to serve as the skeletal frameworks and orientating perspectives into which lexically catalyzed schemas relevant to any content area are placed. They modulate the ways we tie lexically catalyzed schemas to each other in forming propositions, the kinds of time relationships we stipulate among propositions, how we slice action, expectation, and completion, where and how we emphasize, and how detached a perspective we take on the propositions we form.

More generally, the fact that linguistic labels can act, at the individual psychological level, as catalysts to the development of specifically structured perspectives on reality makes it possible for societies to insure not only that their language but also that their institutions, intellectual attainments, and cultural orientations can be passed down from one generation to the next. Certainly speakers build many of the modes of thinking necessary for participation in their culture on the basis of their non-linguistic experience. But their language acts as well, especially in highly abstract realms of thought, as an indispensable tool, guiding them, amidst the vast number of possible integrations of cognitive components in which they could come to think, to develop many of those that participation in their culture requires.

Moreover, once a language has led us to the creation of specific cognitive integrations, no matter how complex they are, or how long it has taken us to build them, we seem to be able to make use of those integrations as tools of our thoughts without any greater investment of cognitive energy than we expend in making use of their simpler components. Once the word ''bachelor'' has led us to integrate the notions man, unmarried, never married, and adult, we are spared the cognitive effort, while thinking about bachelors, of having to keep those four component dimensions, at least consciously-speaking, simultaneously in mind—we are able to think about bachelors, draw up theories about bachelors, and remember things about bachelors as easily as we can think about, draw up theories about, or remember things about men or adults, or unmarried people taken separately. Once we understand the labeled schemas ''society,'' ''phoneme,'' ''methodology,'' or ''acceleration,'' we seem able to entertain those notions directly without having to retrace the cognitive steps by which they were formed, and to make use of them as building blocks of more complex schemas as readily as we make use of such simpler notions as ''red,'' ''chair,'' or ''happy.''

There is no reason, furthermore, to presume that just because linguistic labels have led us to the development of many of the schemas in which we think, that the labels must themselves be present consciously in our mind when we make use of the schemas we owe to them. The point of an art or music appreciation course, a verbal explanation of psychological clinical techniques, in fact, of any instruction aimed at developing thinking structures rather than instilling facts, is to use linguistic labels to encourage the development of cognitive structures that can operate in the absence of the labels through which they have been taught. Teaching the word "perspective" should lead the art student to look at paintings a new way, without the word "perspective" necessarily popping into his mind when he does so. We may very well learn the concept "experimental control" through the word "experimental control." But at a later point when we come to think about how to control the experiments we design or how well other experiments we observe are controlled, we do not seem to require that the words "experimental control" be present as conscious labels for our thoughts. The initial intuitive reaction of a student who has studied linguistics to the question "Is language innate?" is bound to be quite different from the initial intuitive reaction of one who hasn't. The former might easily feel uncomfortable, unable to respond, for the question seems too broad—not because the words "syntax," "semantics," "phonology," etc. are necessarily present in his mind at the moment of his initial intuitive reaction to the question, but presumably because such words have led him to develop a more differentiated model of language in terms of which the question "Is language innate?" is too broad to make sense. We seem to be able to think about a claim made about Behaviorism, without calling any words for a few moments to mind, yet our thinking must be taking place in terms of such notions as "stimulus," "response," "reinforcer," or "control"—in other words, in terms of notions we have developed under the guiding action of labels. Once having mastered the word/concept "moral relativity," we are likely to think about morality or any given set of moral claims, even intuitively, in a different way.

Although then linguistic labels certainly do not act as the medium in which we think, or act to exclusively determine the way in which we think, they do lead us to extend our cognitive repertories in language-specific ways, to develop many schemas through which we come to cognize the world, store information about it and plan our reactions to it that we would be unlikely to develop without their aid.

But the influence of linguistic labels on our cognitive lives appears to extend even beyond the role they play in shaping the schematic foundations of those lives, for linguistic labels not only guide the development of many of our schemas, but they provide those schemas whose development they direct, and specific others besides, with names. And the very fact that a schema is named seems to imply that it can perform some very special cognitive functions that unnamed schemas cannot perform.

LANGUAGE AND THE FUNCTIONING OF
OUR COGNITIVE REPERTORIES

Cognitive Intermediaries of Communication

In the first place, those schemas that our language names serve as the cognitive vehicles through which we must pass our thoughts in order to communicate them in language. We formulate many of the thoughts we intend to communicate within the unlabeled portions of our schematic repertories; but to communicate those thoughts through language we must first "put them into words"—i.e., translate them into schemas that bear labels, pass them through, as it were, that set of structured perspectives on the world for which our particular language provides lexical, grammatical, or intonational names. Similarly, our linguistic messages convey a great deal more information than that represented by their literal meanings—i.e., by the discrete schematic perspectives on reality named by the individual lexical, grammatical, and intonational labels out of which the messages are composed.

But we succeed in understanding these further dimensions of meaning through our understanding of the literal components of the messages themselves. We may, for example, utter the sentence "He plays well" to a good friend and in fact mean by it in context "You'd better not go out for a late drink, but rather get a good night sleep, for the guy you are to play chess with tomorrow is hard to beat." And our friend will very likely understand the full implications of what we had to say by correctly inferring the identity of the person to whom we refer by our use of the pronoun "he," by correctly inferring that our use of the word "play" is meant to signal "play chess" rather than "play tennis," "horse around," or a drama; by correctly inferring that we are being serious and not ironic, and finally by correctly inferring why we are alluding to tomorrow's chess tournament with reference to the present decision about going out for a drink. To accomplish these inferences our friend will certainly call upon many complex schemas that do not have names. But he will be directed to their use—directed to the inferences we intend him to draw—through activation within the labeled portion of his schematic repertory of those schemas whose labels correspond to the words and grammatical structures out of which the message is built (i.e. a schema labeled "he" with a meaning roughly equivalent to "singular, male, person"; a schema labeled "play" with a meaning roughly equivalent to "exercise an enjoyable skill"; a schema labeled "well" with a meaning roughly equivalent to "positive evaluation"; a schema labeled "s" which signals present tense; and a schema labeled by the perceived grammatical structure "noun + verb +

adverb,'' which signifies that the above schemas are to be integrated into an agent/action/manner relational framework.)[21] Analogously, for our friend to understand the sentence, ''Think about the feeling of liberation you get on the first day of vacation'' the way we intend him to understand it, he will have to access a feeling stored in his memory, which does not have a name of its own. But to accomplish this, he will have first to decode the verbal enjoinder by appeal to schemas in his labeled repertory whose labels correspond to the words and grammatical structures out of which it is composed.

We would be severely limited if we could, by our words, only convey literal meanings, if we could communicate only those thoughts that we can represent exclusively in terms of schemas that our language labels. But when we want to communicate by language, we have to call upon those structured perspectives that it labels to act as the intermediaries through which we convert thoughts to labels and through which we convert the labels we hear and read, back to thoughts; and so that select set of schemas that our language labels acts not just as one subset among many within our cognitive repertory, but rather as a very special subset to which we must appeal in every act of linguistic communication.

Accessible Anchors of Mental Perspective

In addition, however, we seem to call upon this very same subset of schemas that our language labels, not only when we want, through language, to give direction to the behavior and thoughts of others, but also when we want to give direction to our own behavior and thoughts. We seem to call specially upon those of our schemas that have names, via their names, when we want to disengage particular schematic perspectives from the collectivity of our interacting associations, ideas, and experiences and make use of those discrete, structured perspectives on reality as stable points of mental orientation to provide direction to our continuing cognitive activities.[22]

We call to mind the linguistic labels ''nutmeg, wax paper, and cottage cheese'' when we want to extract from the collectivity of our thoughts the individuated perspectives on reality those labels name and, thereby, make use of them to orient our shopping behavior. We call to mind the linguistic labels ''lecture, parking, bank, and airport'' so that through the individuated perspectives on reality these labels bring to mind, we can generate a stable mental itinerary for our day's activities. We combine linguistic labels into more complex phrases such as ''the role of labels in shaping thought,'' ''the role of labels in communicating thought,'' and ''the role of labels in guiding thought'' and then, while delivering a lecture,

---

[21]See Bransford & McCarrell, 1974.
[22]See Price, 1953.

call upon these phrases, and hence the composite structured perspectives on reality they label, to provide ourselves with an organizing framework for the development of our argument.[23]

When we want to actively direct our thoughts to a specific topic such as "the recent rise of interest rates" or "What is wrong with the transition paragraph we have just written?" we stipulate the topic to ourselves in words, thereby bringing to mind the discrete perspectives on reality the words label and directing our mental search to those addresses in long term memory where information relevant to the topic at hand is likely to be stored. When we want to focus our thoughts on the question of whether Chomsky's theory of language acquisition can be reconciled with a deterministic view, we first pose the question to ourselves in words, just as we would pose it to someone else, for, by so doing, we bring to mind the individuated perspectives those words name as directive foci for the cognitive processing required to arrive at an appropriate response. When we hit upon an idea that might constitute a relevant response, we try to express it to ourselves in words in order to individuate it and make it in turn the focus of our further analytic and evaluative processes. And if, on the basis of subsequent analyses, we find our idea to be generally correct, but still somehow lacking, we again try to formulate in words what it is that seems lacking in order to isolate a further discrete qualifying hypothesis and enstate it as the next point of orientation of our mental analysis. We feel satisfied when we succeed in putting an idea into words—in translating it into schemas that bear labels—not only because in so doing we succeed in representing it in a form in which it can be readily communicated, but also because in so doing we succeed in differentiating it from the collectivity of our associative ideas, in representing it as a discrete, stable cognitive unit which we can thereafter call upon when we want to direct our mental attention to the specific perspective on the world it represents.

A considerable body of psycholinguistic research points from a variety of perspectives to a similar conclusion with respect to this special contribution which labeled schemas seem to make to cognitive life.

From his studies of psycholinguistic development in children Vygotsky (1962) provides evidence to suggest that only with the development of a facility for actively using word meanings to guide their involvement with the external world are children able to bring individuated property concepts to mind and maintain them in mind as consistent criteria for selecting collec-

---

[23]See Luria (1961, 1968a), Sokolov (1972), Vygotsky (1962), Wozniak (1972), and Zivin (1979) for discussion of the use by young children of external speech as a tool for directing their own behavior, and of the later development of "inner" speech as an internalized tool for performing the same function. See Luria and Yudovich (1959) for discussion of the role played by the development of linguistic skills in development of ability to formulate a project and execute it according to plan, despite intervening distractions; and see Luria (1968b) for discussion of the selective loss of the directive function of speech in certain aphasic patients.

tions of objects; and Luria (1976) provides evidence to suggest an analogous link, among peasants undergoing socialization into Soviet society in the 1930's, between mastery of abstract linguistic terms (e.g., the word "tool") and development of a facility for classifying objects according to the abstract divisions of reality such terms represent. Goldstein (1948) and Zurif and Caramazza (1976) both report a converse relationship among aphasics between language impairment and loss of ability to hold abstract categorical perspectives in mind as bases for classifying objects; and Schwartz, Marin and Saffran (1977) report similar findings among senile dementia patients.[24]

Kendler (1970) presents evidence to suggest that children from the age of five onwards make increasing use of labeled categories as tools for representing to themselves and hence guiding their reactions to the reinforcement contingencies operating in experimental manipulations to which they are exposed. And, conversely, Oléron (1977) reports that language-impaired deaf subjects encounter particular difficulty relative to language-proficient hearing subjects in specifically those tasks that require them first to abstract information from their own task-related activity, and then to make use of that information to direct their continuing task behavior—in tasks, for example, that require them to abstract specific left/right patterns from the responses they have been making and to make use of those patterns as bases for determining their next move, or tasks that require them first abstract the dimension by which they have been classifying a set of objects (e.g., "color" or "shape"), then to abstract a second dimension by which the same objects can be classified, and then to switch from classifying the objects by the first dimension to classifying them by the second.

Moreover, in the cross-cultural arena, Greenfield, Reich, and Olver (1966)[25] report that, in a task virtually identical to this latter one, Wolof-speaking children, who do not have superordinate terms in their lexicon for the notions "color" and "shape," are significantly less proficient at shifting from classifying by one dimension to classifying by the other than are Wolof children who have linguistic command of the superordinate terms "couleur" and "forme" borrowed from French. Having labels for alternative dimensions of classification seems, in other words, to enhance the child's facility for disengaging these alternative dimensions as possible perspectives from which to view the objects displayed before him, and for maintaining these alternative dimensions in mind as points of orientation from which to perform the shifts in classification required.

Clark (1969, 1974) presents evidence to suggest that the words through which one frames a logical problem, by activating specific orienting perspectives on the problem, can significantly affect the ease with which it is solved.[26] And, in a similar vein, Rommetveit (1979) presents evidence to

---

[24]See also Ombredane, 1941.

[25]See also Greenfield and Bruner, 1966.

[26]For instance, the question "If Lee is better than Joe, then who is best?" is appreciably

suggest that the words one uses to define an array of objects to a child, by activating specific orienting perspectives on that array, can significantly affect the child's ability to reason with respect to it.[27]

Beilin and Lust (1975) report a strong correlational link among English-speaking children between the development of accurate understanding and use of the linguisic operator "or"—and therefore, mastery of the abstract perspective on reality to which that label points and with which it remains associated—and the emergence of the cognitive skills necessary to perform at a concrete operational level on Piagetian logical intersection tasks.[28] Similarly Sinclair-de Zwart (1967) reports a correlational link among French-speaking children between development of accurate and spontaneous use of the comparative terms "plus" and "moins" (i.e., more and less) and the emergence of accurate and confident performance on Piagetian conservation and seriation tasks.[29, 30] Sinclair-de Zwart argues that these correlational links do not result from any necessary contribution of the words to task performance, but rather from the fact that the development of a single set of underlying logical structures simultaneously provides the cognitive basis both for mastery of the words and for success on the tasks. However, if one views the words "plus" and "moins" as the linguistic labels of the very schemas used to solve these tasks, it seems reasonable to suppose that the words may have played some role in guiding and even shaping the development of these schemas. And it seems reasonable to suppose as well, that in completing such tasks, the child might make use of the words, not as direct instruments to a solution, but as means of calling to and holding in mind the schemas they name—the very cognitive perspectives the task re-

---

easier to solve than the same question posed as "If Lee isn't as bad as Joe, then who is best?" (See Foss & Hakes [1978] 386–387; Huttenlocher & Higgins [1971]).

[27]Six- to seven-year-olds who were asked, for instance, to point out from an array of six alternative black and white circles of decreasing size "the one of the *snowballs* which is second largest" were considerably more successful than those six- to seven-year-olds who were asked to point out from the same array "the one of the *white circles* which is second largest." According to Rommetveit, the perspective activated by the labeled schema "snowball" facilitated performance for it enabled the children to set immediately aside the irrelevant black circles and concentrate their full attention on the relevant white ones; but the perspective activated by "snowball" in addition reduces the task from one involving three dimensions (i.e. color, circularity and size) to one involving only two dimensions (i.e. snowballness and size) and is likely to have contributed to task performance on that account as well.

[28]Logical intersection involves classifying objects according to two simultaneous dimensions, dividing for instance a collection of large and small, red and white dolls into four piles—the large red, small red, large white, and small white ones.

[29]See Inhelder and Sinclair, 1969, and Sinclair-de Zwart, 1973, for further discussion of the role of linguistic variables in the development of concrete operational skills; and see De Ajuriaguerra and Tissot, (1975) for discussion of the disintegration of concrete operational skills due to language impairment in senile dementia.

[30]For general discussion of concrete operational tasks, see, among others, Cowan, 1978, Flavell, 1963, and Ginsburg and Opper, 1969.

quires; just as an English speaker, while completing a Piagetian conservation of liquid task, might call upon his labeled schema "amount" via its
label, in order to establish as a point of mental orientation an abstract
"amount" of water, which remains constant despite the changing perceptual dimensions of the actual displays of water and which in fact provides
continuity to those perceptual transformations.

Finally, the experimental tradition initiated by Brown and Lenneberg
(1954) represents perhaps the most celebrated attempt to deal experimen-
tally with the impact of linguistic labels on cognitive activity.[31] Brown and
Lenneberg first demonstrated among English-speaking subjects that those
colors which their subjects found easiest to code in language[32] were in fact
the same colors which, after an initial exposure and a time delay, the subjects were best able to recognize from amongst a full array of colors, suggesting that having a short, readily agreed-upon name for a color makes it
easier to form a mental representation of that color and to hold that
representation in mind as a basis for recognizing instances of it. Moreover,
as Brown and Lenneberg increased the time delay between their subjects'
exposure to the colors and the recognition task, the relationship between
linguistic codability and memory increased, suggesting further that the
longer the subject had to hold a color in mind, the weaker any supportive
perceptual encoding of it became and the more he was forced to rely on and
hence become subject to the constraints and conveniences inherent in
whatever linguistic encoding he had available.

Burnham and Clark (1955) soon found, however, that when they exposed
their English-speaking subjects to a more differentiated color array than
that used by Brown and Lenneberg, the colors their subjects remembered
differed markedly from those which Brown and Lenneberg's subjects had
found easiest to encode in English and easiest to remember. These results
brought into question Brown and Lenneberg's interpretation of their own
results, for if those colors which in English have the shortest and most
generally agreed upon names are those which are best remembered, they
should be best remembered whatever the characteristics of the array. But
the use of a highly complex color array requires the subject to make very
fine distinctions in the recognition task, and so it was suggested that
perhaps what counts for facilitating memory at least in such an array is not,
as Brown and Lenneberg had suggested, the ease with which a color is coded
(e.g., how short its name) but rather, more basically, whether one has the
linguistic resources available at all to code that color with sufficient preci-

---

[31]For recent reviews of this work, see Cole and Scribner, 1974, and Rosch, 1977.

[32]The most codable colors were considered to be those upon which there was greatest subject
agreement as to how they should be named—a measure correlated both with the shortness of
the color name and the speed with which subjects were able to access the name.

sion so as to be able to distinguish it effectively from competing colors in the recognition array.[33]

Lantz and Stefflre (1964) provided strong support for this revised position by demonstrating, both for the color array used by Brown and Lenneberg and for that used by Burnham and Clark, a significant relationship between "communication accuracy"—i.e., the accuracy with which a speaker can designate a specific shade of color to another speaker of his language via a linguistic description, regardless of the complexity of that description—and color memory; and Stefflre, Vales, and Morley (1966) found, for both a group of Spanish-speakers and a group of Yucatec-speakers from the same region of Mexico, not only that the colors that each group most accurately communicated were those they best remembered, but also that the colors that were most accurately communicated and best remembered by the Spanish-speakers differed from those that were most accurately communicated and best remembered by the Yucatec-speakers. Furthermore, Lenneberg and Roberts (1953) had found that Zuni speakers who do not have available distinct terms for yellow and orange in their color lexicons frequently confused yellow and orange samples in color recognition tasks, while monolingual English-speaking subjects never made that confusion, and while bilingual Zunis who knew English fell between the monolingual Zunis and the monolingual English speakers. And Greenfield, Reich, and Olver (1966) reported virtually identical findings with respect to the same color distinction from monolingual Wolof speakers, Wolofs who knew French, and monolingual French speakers.[34] So, within the developing color-memory tradition, availability of linguistic resources for precise encoding had replaced ease of codability as the linguistic variable seen to have the most important and consistent impact on color memory, but the fact that linguistic labels play a role in facilitating color memory seemed well established.

Then a new challenge arose to the color-memory work in the form of evidence provided by Berlin and Kay (1969) and Rosch (1973, 1977) to suggest that certain "focal" color areas within the color spectrum are universally best remembered, whether or not speakers have names for them, because of a special salience which the human perceptual system seems to bestow upon them. Further evidence indicated, moreover, that these universally salient focal colors tend across languages to come to have the most easily codable names, leading to the suggestion that the correlation that

---

[33]See Lenneberg, 1967.

[34]Interestingly, Poeck and Stachowiak (1975) and Wyke and Holgate (1973; see also Lesser, 1978) from independent studies both report that language impairment due to aphasia seems to have a particularly debilitating effect on subject ability to work with the category "orange" as compared to more primary colors, often in fact resulting in a confounding of the orange/yellow distinction.

Brown and Lenneberg had originally found between ease of codability and memory might be artifactual, resulting not from any impact of linguistic codability on color memory, but rather from the fact that Brown and Lenneberg were tapping perceptually salient colors which, for that reason, were both easier to encode in language and easier to remember.[35] However, the existence of a small universal set of highly salient colors cannot explain the fact that in the original Brown and Lenneberg experiment, as the experimenters increased the time delay between their subjects' exposure to the colors and the recognition task, the relationship between linguistic codability and memory increased. Nor can it explain the fact that in the Lenneberg and Roberts; Greenfield, Reich and Olver; and Stefflre, Vales and Morley experiments, those colors which were best named, or best communicated, and best remembered differed for speakers of different languages. And in more general terms, even if their exists a small set of universally salient colors, as one moves beyond that set to color categories like "chartreuse," "mauve," "crimson," or even "orange," there is no reason to presume that linguistic labels do not begin to play more important cognitive roles in furnishing speakers with effective supplementary means for holding distinctly in mind the specific portions of the color spectrum that they label.[36]

The existence of a small universal set of highly salient colors might explain or explain in part the correlation found in the original Brown and Lenneberg experiment, and it certainly suggests that the effects of linguistic labels on the formation of color categories and on the retention of colors in memory have to be understood as operating within a limiting context defined by those effects that derive from the characteristics of the human perceptual system. But it by no means undercuts the principal claim of the color-memory tradition that a subject's ability to remember a color can be influenced by his ability to code that color in his language.

Ironically, the most serious weakness of the color-memory tradition does not stem either from the fact that it originally selected as its independent variable the ease, rather than the precision, with which a color can be coded in a particular language, nor from the fact that universal perceptual patterns of salience may account for some of its results. The color-memory tradition sought to uncover linguistic effects on thinking in just those areas and in just those kinds of tasks in which such effects might be expected to be both least pronounced and hardest to demonstrate.[37] It is precisely in perceptually tied areas such as color categorization where speakers are most likely to develop schematic divisions of reality independently of language and hence where they should be least subject to the constraints and conveniences inherent in the way their language happens to divide up the world.

---

[35]See Rosch, 1977.

[36]See Greenfield and Childs, 1974, as cited in Rosch, 1977.

[37]See also Carrol and Casagrande, 1958; and Mori, 1976.

And it is precisely in tasks such as those of color memory, in which speakers can make use of direct perceptual encodings, that they should feel the least need to call upon the special services their labeled schemas provide and hence be least affected in their task performance by the constraints and conveniences inherent in that specific subset of schemas for which their language provides names. That the findings of the color-memory tradition were significant at all only testifies to the strength and pervasiveness of the impact of language on our thoughts—an impact whose effects seem to appear even within that area of cognition and even in those kinds of tasks in which we have reason to expect that they would be most overwhelmed by non-linguistic variables.

The theoretical framework advanced in this book and the experimental findings offered in support of it lead then to the conclusion that distinct languages, by labeling certain perspectives on reality as opposed to others, act (1) to encourage their speakers to extend their repertories of cognitive schemas in language-specific ways and (2) to define for their speakers that particular set of schemas they can make use of to mediate their linguistic acts and to establish explicit points of mental orientation for giving direction to their thoughts.

If, moreover, we are to uncover the more significant effects of language on the way we think, we have to turn our attention away from the cognitive effects of linguistic labels, such as color names, that stake out simple categorizations of the perceptual world, and direct our attention instead to the cognitive effects of linguistic labels that lead us to build those highly complex, abstractly derived perspectives on reality that we unlikely to construct without their aid. We have to turn our attention, in other words, to the cognitive effects of such lexical labels as "amount," "money supply," and "Existentialism," and to the cognitive effects of such grammatical labels as "if-and-only-if-then," "if X had been . . . then Y would have been . . . ," and "the contribution of X to the relationship between an entified Y and an entified Z." And we have to turn our attention as well, away from tasks such as those of color memory in which perceptual encodings of task relevant information can compete with, or substitute for, linguistic encodings, and direct our attention instead to tasks in which successful performance depends on the use of information that can neither be represented in perceptual terms nor easily disengaged and maintained in mind without the aid of associated linguistic labels. We have to turn our attention, in other words, to tasks such as those which require subjects to assume and operate with counterfactual or entified/relational, theoretical perspectives on the world. It is difficult to imagine how, without distinct labels to name them, we could disengage from the collectivity of our thoughts such specific perspectives as "If Bier had been able to speak Chinese, he would have made lasting contributions to the development of Western philosophy" or "The contribution of high altitude to the relationship between living in a polluted environment and getting lung disease." And it is difficult to imagine how, without distinct labels to name them, we could make use of these perspectives as stable points of mental orientation for giving direction to our further cognitive activity. In light, then, of the picture presented in this chapter of the role language plays in the development and functioning of our thoughts, the areas of cognition studied in the investigation reported in Chapter 1 and the tasks used to study them should constitute examples of the kinds of cognitive areas and the kinds of cognitive tasks in which the more dramatic and significant effects of language on thought are likely to emerge.[38]

COGNITIVE BARRIERS TO CROSS-LINGUISTIC COMMUNICATION

Speakers of distinct languages, despite the linguistic differences which separate them, as human beings, build their cognitive repertories on the basis of similar genetic endowments, similar sensory, motor and intellectual capacities, and in many respects similar environmental experiences, and so come to cognize the world in many similar ways. They likewise borrow labeled schemas from each other and develop labeled schemas of their own to match those of others, and thereby further expand the cognitive terrain which they share. So, although speakers of distinct languages may differ in what they label and in what labels they use, they still come to hold a great many cognitive schemas in common and thus to share the cognitive bases they need to communicate to each other, via translation, a great deal of what they mean.

---

[38]In a recent book, Laitin (1977) presents evidence from native Somali, Somali-English bilinguals of a readiness to adopt distinct attitudinal orientations when using one of their languages as opposed to the other. The bilingual subjects are asked to role-play specified situations in either Somali or in English; and which language they are asked to use turns out to be closely related to such things as how they characterize their own nationality status, how they react to authority figures, what kind of argument style they employ and how many religious values enter their conversation. In an experiment in the same tradition, Ervin-Tripp (1973) asked a native Japanese, Japanese-English bilingual to interpret a set of pictures, at one point using Japanese and at another point using English. She found that when the subject was asked to respond in his native Japanese as opposed to English, he consistently offered interpretations of more emotional and more achievement-oriented content. These kinds of studies do not seek to clarify the specific components of the language responsible for whatever effects are observed, nor do they seek to distinguish the purely cognitive effects a language might have at the level of individual cognitive schemas either from the broad attitudinal effects to which those cognitive effects may in turn give rise, or from the cognitive or behavioral associations one language as opposed to another may gather for a bilingual as a result of where, when, with whom, in what cultural context it is spoken. Therefore, although such studies are highly interesting in themselves, they are only tangentially relevant to present concerns.

If the thoughts of a speaker of language A can be represented in labeled schemas of his language for which equivalent or nearly equivalent labeled schemas exist in language B, he has merely to stipulate those equivalents in order to translate his thoughts into that other linguistic world. But even if his thoughts cannot be directly represented in labeled schemas in one or both languages, as long as they can be understood in terms of cognitive schemas which the speakers of both languages share, translation can still go through. The speaker of language A can make use of labeled schemas that have equivalents in language B to induce the speaker of language B to call to mind the intended thoughts, just as the speaker of English, by referring to "that feeling of liberation you get on the first day of vacation" induces his fellow English speaker to call to mind a feeling both speakers have experienced and stored, but for which neither speaker has a name.

But when a speaker of language A labels a specific perspective on the world which the speaker of language B not only does not label, but also does not share, then translation cannot proceed by simply supplying a suggestive circumlocution. Translation can then fully succeed only if it can induce the speaker of language B not to call upon, but rather to construct, a cognitive schema of the parameters required. If the labeled schema of language A represents an easily apprehendible categorization of the perceptual world that the speaker of language B has simply not yet had the opportunity to experience—as might for instance be the case with respect to a labeled schema for a specific type of Japanese screen, Chinese tea, Mexican pepper, or Thai fruit—than a simple pictorial representation, or a simple taste, or a simple verbal description may convey sufficient information for the speaker of language B to construct on the spot a schema of the degree of precision required. If the labeled schema of language A is more abstract, but can be readily constructed out of a combination of labeled schemas that the speaker of language B has available—as in the case, for instance, of translation into English of the distinct Chinese terms for "oldest brother," "older brothers," "father's older brother," and "father's younger brothers"—then, again through the virtually immediate construction of the schematic perspective on reality involved, the speaker of language B can come to understand what the speaker of language A means. But an English speaker cannot rely on a taste of experience, or a brief verbal description, or a simple combination of labeled schemas from his repertory, to understand what a French speaker means by "apprécier" by contrast to what he himself means by the verb "to appreciate"; to understand what the Chinese speaker means by "li mao"—with its moral and natural law implications—by contrast to what he means by its rough English translation equivalent "etiquette"—with its social and conventional implications—; or to understand the highly subtle distinctions carried by the more than ten Chinese terms which divide up the semantic range of the English noun "reason" or the highly subtle distinctions in level of formality signalled by the various Japanese terms that serve in the place of the English "you".[39] One cannot simply translate into English what the Portuguese mean by their marvelous word "saudades," which combines nostalgia with love and loneliness; or into non-technical English what linguists mean by "transformation," what philosophers mean by "quantifier," or what stockbrokers mean by "put," or "call," anymore than one can simply translate into Chinese what "would have" or "theoretical"—in the severing of truth-commitment sense—mean. What is required in each case is not simply translation, but a complex cognitive accomplishment—an accomplishment that may be aided by appeal to categories the speaker already has and by appeal to exemplar situations that he has experienced—but an accomplishment that must in addition involve mastering, under the direction of linguistic labels, a new mode of thought—an accomplishment that, on a more abstract level, is analogous to Johnny's construction of an appropriate labeled schema for "amount."

By intervening in highly abstract realms of thought to shape their speakers' cognitive lives, languages act to insure the maintenance across generations of the most complex cognitive attainments of the human race and of the most complex cognitive attainments of its individual cultures. But, ironically, these same cognitive contributions act to separate their speakers cognitively from speakers of other languages—to create and perpetuate significant cognitive barriers to cross-linguistic communication and understanding. The barriers are certainly not impenetrable. But to penetrate them one cannot rely simply on a translation equivalent or a convenient paraphrase. Here, in highly abstract realms of thought, translation depends on, and provides the direction for, cognitive growth.

REFERENCES

Ayer, A.J. *Language, truth and logic*. London: Gollancz, 1936.

Beilin, H., & Lust, B. A study in the development of logical and linguistic connectives: Cognitive data and summary. In H. Beilin (Ed.), *Studies in the cognitive basis of language development*. New York: Academic Press, 1975.

Berlin, B., & Kay, P. *Basic color terms: Their universality and evolution*. Berkeley: University of California Press, 1969.

Bever, T. The cognitive basis for linguistic structures. In J. J. Hayes (Ed.), *Cognition and the development of language*. New York: Wiley, 1970.

Blank, M. Mastering the intangible through language. In D. Aaronson & R. W. Rieber (Eds.), *Developmental psycholinguistics and communicative disorders*. New York: New York Academy of Sciences, 1975. (Annals of the New York Academy of Sciences, Vol. 263.)

Bloom, A. H. Two dimensions of moral reasoning: Social principledness and social humanism in cross-cultural perspective. *Journal of Social Psychology*, 1977, *101*, 29–44. (a)

Bloom, A. H. A cognitive dimension of social control: The Hong Kong Chinese in cross-

---

[39]See Suzuki, 1978.

cultural perspective. In A. A. Wilson, S. L. Greenblatt, & R. W. Wilson (Eds), *Deviance and social control in Chinese society.* New York: Praeger Publishers, 1977. (b)

Bloom, A. H. The role of the Chinese language in counterfactual/theoretical thinking and evaluation. In R. W. Wilson, A. A. Wilson, & S. L. Greenblatt (Eds), *Value change in Chinese society.* New York: Praeger, 1979. (a)

Bloom, A. H. The impact of Chinese linguistic structure on cognitive style. *Current Anthropology,* September, 1979, *20,* (3), 585. (b)

Bloomfield, L. *Language.* New York: Holt, Rinehart & Winston, 1933.

Bransford, J. D., & McCarrell, N. S. A sketch of a cognitive approach to comprehension: Some thoughts about understanding what it means to comprehend. In W. B. Weimer & D. S. Palermo (Eds.) *Cognition and the symbolic process.* Hillsdale, N.J.: Lawrence Erlbaum Associates, 1974.

Brewer, W. F. There is no convincing evidence for operant or classical conditioning in adult humans. In W. B. Weimer & D. S. Palermo (Eds), *Cognition and the symbolic process.* Hillsdale, N.J.: Lawrence Erlbaum Associates, 1974.

Brown, R. *Words and things: An introduction to language.* New York: Free Press, 1958.

Brown, R. *Psycholinguistics: Selected papers.* New York: Free Press, 1970.

Brown, R. *A First language: The early stages.* Cambridge, Mass.: Harvard University Press, 1973.

Brown, R., & Lenneberg, E. A study in language and cognition. *Journal of Abnormal and Social Psychology,* 1954, *49,* 454–462.

Burnham, R. W., & Clark, J. R. A test of hue memory. *Journal of Applied Psychology,* 1955, *39,* 164–172.

Carroll, J. B., & Casagrande, J. B. The function of language classification. In E. E. Maccoby *et al.* (Eds.), *Readings in social psychology.* New York: Holt, Rinehart & Winston, 1958.

Chan, W. T. *A source book in Chinese philosophy.* Princeton, N.J.: Princeton University Press, 1963.

Chao, Y. R. *A grammar of spoken Chinese.* Berkeley: University of California Press, 1968.

Chomsky, N. *Syntactic structures.* The Hague: Mouton, 1957.

Chomsky, N. A review of B. F. Skinner's verbal behavior. *Language,* 1959, *35* (1), 26–58.

Chomsky, N. *Aspects of the theory of syntax.* Cambridge, Mass.: MIT Press, 1965.

Chomsky, N. *Language and mind.* New York: Harcourt, Brace & Jovanovitch, 1968.

Chomsky, N. Remarks on nominalization. In N. Chomsky, *Studies on semantics in generative grammar.* The Hague: Mouton, 1972.

Chomsky, N. *Reflections on language.* New York: Pantheon, 1975.

Clark, E. V. What's in a word? On the child's acquisition of semantics in his first language. In T. E. Moore (Ed.), *Cognitive development and the acquisition of language.* New York: Academic Press, 1973.

Clark, H. H. Linguistic processes in deductive reasoning. *Psychological Review,* 1969, *76,* 387–404.

Clark, H. H. Semantics and comprehension. In T. A. Sebeok (Ed.), *Current trends in linguistics, Vol. 12: Linguistics and adjacent arts and sciences.* The Hague: Mouton, 1974.

Clark, H. H., & Clark, E. V. *Psychology and language: An introduction to psycholinguistics.* New York: Harcourt, Brace & Jovanovitch, 1977.

Cole, M., Gay, J., Glick, J. A., & Sharp, D. W. *The cultural context of learning and thinking: An exploration in experimental anthropology.* New York: Basic Books, 1971.

Cole, M., & Scribner, S. *Culture and thought: A psychological introduction.* New York: Wiley, 1974.

Collins, A. M., & Loftus, E. F. A spreading activation theory of semantic processing. *Psychological Review,* 1975, *82* (6), 407–428.

Cowan, P. *Piaget: With feeling—Cognitive, social, and emotional dimensions.* New York: Holt, Rinehart & Winston, 1978.

Crick, M. *Explorations in language and meaning: Towards a semantic anthropology.* London: Malaby Press, 1976.

De Ajuriaguerra, J., & Tissot, R. Language in senile dementia. In E. H. Lenneberg & E. Lenneberg (Eds.), *Foundations of language development: A multidisciplinary approach, Vol. I.* New York: Academic Press, 1975.

Earle, M. Bilingual semantic merging and an aspect of acculturation. *Journal of Personality and Social Psychology*, 1967, *6*, 304–312.

Ervin-Tripp, S. M. *Language acquisition and communicative choice.* Stanford, Calif.: Stanford University Press, 1973.

Ferguson, C., & Slobin, D. (Eds). *Studies of child language development.* New York: Holt, Rinehart, & Winston, 1973.

Flavell, J. *The developmental psychology of Jean Piaget.* New York: Van Nostrand Reinhold, 1963.

Fodor, J. A. *The Language of thought.* New York; Thomas Y. Crowell, 1975.

Foss, D. J., & Hakes, D. T. *Psycholinguistics: An introduction to the psychology of language.* Englewood Cliffs, N. J.: Prentice-Hall, 1978.

Frege, G. On sense and reference. In P. Geach & M. Black (Eds.), *Philosophical writings of Gottlob Frege.* Oxford: Basil Blackwell, 1960 [Original edition, 1892].

Fromkin, V. A. Slips of the tongue. *Scientific American*, December, 1973, *229*, 110–116.

Fung, Y. L. *A History of Chinese philosophy.* Princeton, N.J.: Princeton University Press, 1952.

Ginsburg, H., & Opper, S. *Piaget's theory of intellectual development: An introduction.* Englewood Cliffs, N.J.: Prentice-Hall, 1969.

Goldstein, K. *Language and Language disturbance.* New York: Grune & Stratton, 1948.

Granet, M. *La pensée chinoise.* Paris. Renaissance du Livre, 1934.

Greenfield, P. M., & Bruner, J. S. Culture and cognitive growth. *International Journal of Psychology*, 1966, *1*, 89–107.

Greenfield, P. M., & Childs, C. Weaving, color terms, and pattern representation: Cultural influences and cognitive development among the Zinacantecos of southern Mexico. In J. Dawson & W. Lonner (Eds), *Readings in cross-cultural psychology: Proceedings of the First International Conference of the International Association for Cross-Cultural Psychology.* Hong Kong: University of Hong Kong Press., as cited in Rosch, E., Linguistic Relativity. In P. N. Johnson-Laird & P. C. Wason (Eds.), *Thinking: Readings in cognitive science*, Cambridge: Cambridge University Press, 1977.

Greenfield, P. M., Reich, L. C., & Olver, R. R. On culture and equivalence: II. In J. S. Bruner, R. R. Olver, & P. M. Greenfield *et al.*, *Studies in cognitive growth.* New York: Wiley, 1966.

Greenfield, P. M., & Smith, J. H. *The structure of communication in early language development.* New York: Academic Press, 1976.

Harris, Z. S. *Methods in structural linguistics.* Chicago: University of Chicago Press, 1951.

Hoijer, H. (Ed.) *Language and culture.* Chicago: University of Chicago Press, 1954.

Hu Shih. *Development of the logical method in ancient China.* New York: Paragon Books, 1963.

Humbolt, W. V. *Gesammelte schriften.* A. Leitzmann (Ed.), Berlin: B. Behrs Verlag, 1903–1918.

Huttenlocher, J., & Higgins, E. T. Adjectives, comparatives, and syllogisms. *Psychological Review*, 1971, *78*, 487-504.

Inhelder, B., & Sinclair, H. Learning cognitive structures. In P. Mussen, J. Langer, & M. Covington. *Trends and issues in developmental psychology.* New York: Holt, Rinehart & Winston, 1969.

Katz, J. J. A proper theory of names. *Philosophical Studies*, 1944, *31*, 1–80.

Katz, J. J. *Semantic Theory.* New York: Harper & Row, 1972.

Katz, J. J., & Postal, P. M. *An integrated theory of linguistic descriptions.* Cambridge, Mass.: MIT Press, 1964.

Kelman, H. C. Violence without moral restraint: Reflections on the dehumanization of victims and victimizers. *Journal of Social Issues*, 1973, *29*, (4), 25-61.

Kendler, T. Development of mediating responses in children. In P. Mussen, J. Conger, & J. Kagan (Eds.), *Readings in child development and personality.* New York: Harper & Row, 1970.

Kintsch, W. *The representation of meaning in memory.* Hillsdale, N. J.: Lawrence Erlbaum Associates, 1974.

Kohlberg, L. Stage and sequence: The cognitive developmental approach to socialization. In D. A. Goslin (Ed.), *Handbook of socialization theory and research.* Chicago: Rand McNally, 1969.

Kohlberg, L. From is to ought: How to commit the naturalistic fallacy and get away with it in the study of moral development. In T. Mischel (Ed.), *Cognitive development and Epistemology.* New York: Academic Press, 1971.

Laitin, D. D. *Politics, language and thought: The Somali experience.* Chicago: University of Chicago Press, 1977.

Lantz, D., & Stefflre, V. Language and cognition revisited. *Journal of Abnormal and Social Psychology*, 1964, *69*, 472-481.

Lenneberg, E. H. *Biological foundations of language.* New York: Wiley, 1967.

Lenneberg, E. H., & Roberts, J. M. *The detonata of color terms.* Paper read at Linguistic Society of America, Bloomington, Indiana, August, 1953, as cited in Brown, R & Lenneberg, E., A study in language and cognition. *Journal of Abnormal and Social Psychology*, 1954, *49*, 454-462.

Lesser, R. *Linguistic investigations of aphasia.* London: Edward Arnold, 1978.

Levenson, J. R. *Confucian China and its modern fate.* Berkeley: University of California Press, 1965.

Lickona, T. (Ed.) *Moral development and behavior: Theory, research and social issues.* New York: Holt, Rinehart & Winston, 1976.

Luria, A. R. *The Role of speech in the regulation of normal and abnormal behavior.* New York: Liveright, 1961.

Luria, A. R. The directive function of speech in development and dissolution, Part I. In R. C. Oldfield & J. C. Marshall, (Eds.) *Language.* Baltimore: Penguin Books, 1968. (a)

Luria, A. R. The directive function of speech in development and dissolution, Part II. In R. C. Oldfield & J. C. Marshall, (Eds.), *Language.* Baltimore: Penguin, 1968. (b)

Luria, A. R. *Cognitive development: Its cultural and social foundations.* Cambridge, Mass.: Harvard University Press, 1976.

Luria, A. R., & Yudovich, F. *Speech and the development of mental processes in the child: An experimental investigation.* London; Staples Press, 1959.

Macnamara, J. Cognitive basis of language learning in infants. *Psychology Review*, 1972, *79* (1), 1-12.

Macnamara, J. *Language learning and thought.* New York Academic Press, 1977.

Malraux, A. *The temptation of the West.* New York: Random House, 1961 [Original French edition, 1926].

Maratsos, M. P. *The use of definite and indefinite reference in young children: An experimental study in semantic acquisition.* Cambridge: Cambridge University Press, 1976.

Mori, I. A cross-cultural study on children's conception of speed and duration: A comparison between Japanese and Thai children. *Japanese Psychological Research*, 1976, *18*, (3), 105-112.

Needham, J. *Science and civilization in China, Vol. 2: History of scientific thought.*

Cambridge: Cambridge University Press, 1956.

Needham, J. *Science and civilization in China, Vol. 3: Mathematics and the sciences of the heavens and the earth.* Cambridge: Cambridge University Press, 1959.

Northrop, F. S. C. *The meeting of East and West.* New York: MacMillan, 1946.

Oléron, P. *Language and mental development.* Hillsdale, N.J.: Lawrence Elrbaum Associates, 1977.

Ombredane, A. *L'aphasie et l' élaboration de la pensée explicite.* Paris: Presses Universitaires de France, 1941.

Piaget, J. *The language and thought of the child.* New York: Harcourt, Brace, 1926.

Piaget, J. *The origins of intelligence in the child.* New York: International University Press, 1952.

Piaget, J. *The Psychology of Intelligence.* Totowa, N.J.: Littlefield, Adams, 1960.

Piaget, J. *Biology and knowledge.* Chicago: University of Chicago Press, 1971.

Piaget, J., & Inhelder, B. *The psychology of the child.* New York: Basic Books, 1969.

Plotkin, H. *Noun usage in Chinese and English: A comparative study in language and thought.* Unpublished senior paper. Swarthmore College, 1977.

Poeck, R., & Stachowiak, F. J. Farbennungsstorungen bei aphasischen und nichtaphasischen hirnkranken. *Journal of Neurology,* 1975, *209,* 95–102.

Price, H. H. *Thinking and experience.* London: Hutchinson University Library, 1953.

Putnam, H. The analytic and the synthetic. In J. F. Rosenberg & C. Travis (Eds), *Readings in the philosophy of language.* Englewood Cliffs, N. J.: Prentice-Hall, 1971.

Quine, W. V. O. *Word and object.* Cambridge, Mass.: MIT Press, 1960.

Rommetveit, R. On the relationship between children's mastery of Piagetian cognitive operations and their semantic competence. In R. Rommetveit & R. M. Blakar (Eds.), *Studies of language, thought and verbal communication.* London: Academic Press, 1979.

Romney, A. K., & D'Andrade, R. G. (Eds). *Transcultural studies in Cognition. American Anthropologist,* Part 2 1964, *66* (3).

Rosch, E. On the internal structure of perceptual and semantic categories. In T. E. Moore (Ed.), *Cognitive development and the acquisition of language.* New York: Academic Press, 1973.

Rosch, E. Linguistic relativity. In P. N. Johnson-Laird & P. C. Wason (Eds.), *Thinking: Readings in cognitive science.* Cambridge: Cambridge University Press, 1977.

Rosch, E. Principles of categorization. In E. Rosch & B. Lloyd (Eds.), *Cognition and categorization.* Hillsdale, N.J.: Lawrence Erlbaum Associates, 1978.

Rumelhart, D. E., Lindsay, P. H., & Norman, D. A. A process model for long-term memory. In E. Tulving & W. Donaldson (Eds.), *Organization of memory.* New York: Academic Press, 1972.

Russell, B. On denoting. *Mind.* 1905, *14,* 479–493.

Sanford, N., Comstock, C., *et al. Sanctions for evil.* San Francisco: Jossey-Bass, 1971.

Sapir, E. *Language: An Introduction to the Study of Speech.* New York: Harcourt, Brace, 1921.

Scribner, S. Modes of thinking and ways of speaking: Culture and logic reconsidered. In P. N. Johnson-Laird & P. C. Wason (Eds.), *Thinking: Readings in cognitive science.* Cambridge: Cambridge University Press, 1977.

Schwartz, M., Marin, O., & Saffran, E. *Language and reference in dementia: A case study.* Unpublished manuscript, 1977.

Searle, J. *Speech acts.* Cambridge: Cambridge University Press, 1969.

Sinclair-de Zwart, H. *Acquisition du language et développement de la pensée: Sous-systèmes linguistiques et opérations concrètes.* Paris: Dunod, 1967.

Sinclair-de Zwart, H. Language acquisition and cognitive development. In T. E. Moore (Ed.), *Cognitive development and the acquisition of language.* New York: Academic Press, 1973.

Sivin, N. Wang Hsi-shan. In *Dictionary of scientific biography*, New York: Scribner, 1970, *14*, 159-168.

Slobin, D. I. *Psycholinguistics, 2nd Edition*. Glenville, Ill.: Scott, Foresman, 1979.

Smith, E., Shoben, E. J., & Rips, L. J. Structure and process in semantic memory: A featural model for semantic decisions. *Psychological Review*, 1974, *81* (3), 214-241.

Sokolov, A. N. *Inner speech and thought*. New York: Plenum, 1972.

Stefflre, V., Vales, V. C., & Morley, L. Language and cognition in Yucatan: A cross-cultural replication. *Journal of Personality and Social Psychology*, 1966, *4* (1), 112-115.

Suzuki, T. *Japanese and the Japanese: Words in culture*. Tokyo: Kodansha, 1978.

Taylor, I. *Introduction to psycholinguistics*. New York: Holt, Rinehart & Winston, 1976.

Tulving, E. Episodic and semantic memory. In E. Tulving & W. Donaldson (Eds.), *Organization of memory*. New York: Academic Press, 1972.

Vygotsky, L. S. *Thought and language*. Cambridge, Mass.: MIT Press, 1962.

Weinreich, U. *Languages in contact*. Paris: Mouton, 1968.

Whorf, B. L. *Language, thought and reality*. Cambridge, Mass. MIT Press, 1956.

Winograd, T. Formalisms for knowledge. In P. N. Johnson-Laird & P. C. Wason (Eds.), *Thinking: Readings in cognitive science*. Cambridge University Press, 1977.

Wittgenstein, J. *Philosophical investigations*. New York: MacMillan, 1953.

Wozniak, R. I. Verbal regulation of motor behavior: Soviet research and non-Soviet replications. *Human Development*, 1972, *15*, 13-57.

Wyke, M., & Holgate, D. Color naming defects in dyphasic patients: A qualitative analysis. *Neuropsychologia*, 1973, *11*, 451-461.

Zivin, G. (Ed.), *The development of self-regulation through private speech*. New York: Wiley, 1979.

Zurif, E. B., & Caramazza, A. Psycholinguistic structures in aphasia. In H. Whitaker & H. A. Whitaker (Eds.), *Studies in neurolinguistics, Vol. I.*. New York: Academic Press, 1976.

APPENDIX

A. Counterfactual Stories: Original Versions

古代有一位不會中文的希臘哲學家,名叫 德哥。假如他會中文,因為那個時候中國跟希臘有貿易來往,因此他受到中國文化的影响,他知道中國跟希臘的邏輯學各有所長,他把中國那個時期的邏輯學跟希臘那個時期的邏輯學溶化為一体,創造一個進步的新邏輯學,這將对中國跟希臘的哲學進步有很大的貢廳尤。

　　由上面這个故事内容来看,在下列的四个問題之中,請您告訴我们那個(那些)是您認为有道理的问题。請不要回答,只在每個问題後頭,把有道理或是沒道理圈出来就尤可以了。

a. 德哥在哲学發展中有什加貢献? <u>有道理</u>　　沒道理

b. 德哥的貢献有多应重要? <u>有道理</u>　　沒道理

c. 德哥怎应可以受到中國邏輯學的影响. <u>有道理</u>　　沒道理

d. 什应條件能促使他成为一個有各的哲学家? <u>有道理</u>　　沒道理

A. Counterfactual Stories: Original Versions (cont.)

In ancient times there was a Greek philosopher who didn't know any Chinese, by the name of Decos. If he had known Chinese, because at that time China and Greece had a trading relationship, he would have been influenced by Chinese culture. He would have found out the best points of Greek and Chinese logic and integrated the Greek logic and Chinese logic of that time to create a new advanced logic which would have made a very large contribution to the development of both Greek and Chinese philosophy.

With reference to the content of the above, answer the following questions. If you think a question doesn't make sense, please explain why.

A. What kind of contribution did Decos make to the development of philosophy?
B. How important was Decos' contribution?
C. Only under what condition would Decos have been able to make a contribution to Chinese and Greek logic?

A. Counterfactual Stories: Original Versions (cont.)

請您圈出下面句故事有関的幾個問題的正確答案。謝謝您跟我们合作。

故事：某一個國家大約在二十年以前，他们与世界上其他的國家関係完全斷絶了。因此世界上其他國家立刻把援助都停止了。如果那個國家没那樣做，一方面在那二十年之中外國人有機會去觀光句做買賣，那個國家的人民也有機會到外國去觀摩，因此那個國家就不能維持他们自己的傳統習慣了。另一方面在經濟上得到很多的援助句外匯，那就就使那個國家由農業國家發展為工業國家。

問題：a 那個國家的人民在那二十年之中是否与其他國家人民有来往？

　　　A. 有来往　　　　　　B. 没有来往

　　b. 那個國家在傳統習慣基礎上改變了没有？

　　　A. 改變了　　　　　　B. 没改變

　　C. 那個國家已經成為工業國家了没有？

　　　A. 成為工業國家了　　B. 還是農業國家。

A. Counterfactual Stories: Original Versions (Cont.)

About twenty years ago, a certain nation completely broke off relations with the rest of the world. Because of this all nations immediately cut off all foreign assistance to it. If that nation hadn't acted as it had, foreigners would have had, over the past twenty years, the opportunity to visit and do business there and that nation's people would have had the opportunity to visit other nations and observe them. As a result it could not have maintained its traditions and habits. From an economic point of view, however, it would have received a great deal of foreign aid and foreign capital, which would have made it possible for that nation to develop from an agricultural to an industrialized nation.

1. In the past twenty years did this nation's people receive visitors from other nations and visit other nations?

      Yes   No

2. Did the traditions and habits of this nation change fundamentally over the past twenty years?

      Yes   No

3. Has this country already become an industrialized nation?

      Yes   No.

A. Counterfactual Stories: Version Two
(See text for English Version)

畢爾是十八世紀的德國哲學家，他很喜歡研究大同世界的道理以及自然的法則，因為那個時候中國跟歐洲已經有相當的來往，中國的哲學著作可以在歐洲看到，但是經過翻譯的却很少。畢爾他不會看中國字，可是如果他會看的話，他就一定發現那些中國哲學家的作品，跟他所主張的學說很有關係。尤其最影響他的就是中國哲學家在描寫自然現象的時候，習慣注意到自然現象互相的關係。因為這個看法跟那個時代的歐洲哲學家，習慣把自然現象抽出來單獨描寫完全相反，所以畢爾受到這種看法的影響以後，才把中國跟西方的哲學混合在一起，創造一個注意到自然現象的本性，同時也注意到自然現象互相關係的哲學理論，來補足那一代西方哲學的缺點，並且深深的影響了德國、法國跟荷蘭的哲學家，而使西方的哲學更進一步，同時也使哲學更接近了科學。

(1)從上面的這篇短文來看畢爾對哲學的發展有什麼貢獻呢？

(2)最影響畢爾的是什麼？

A. Counterfactual Stories: Version Three

畢爾是十八世紀的德國哲學家，他很喜歡研究大同世界的道理以及自然的法則。那個時候中國跟歐洲已經有相當的來往，中國的著作也可以在歐洲看到，可是還沒有翻成外文的。畢爾不會看中文，如果會看的話，一定會發現中國哲學家在描寫自然現象的時候，往往注意到自然現象相互的關係，而那個時代的歐洲哲學家，往往把自然現象隔離，單獨研究。如果畢爾讀過中國哲學的話，一定會受到中國哲學家的影響，把中國跟西方的哲學融合在一起，創造一個哲學理論不僅可以研究自然現象的本質也可以把這些自然現象之間的關係解釋清楚，這個理論不但會補足那個時代西方哲學的缺點，並且也會深深的影響德國、法國跟荷蘭的哲學，使它更接近科學。

從上面這篇文章請問你畢爾給西方帶來什麼新的影響？（請你在下面的幾個答案裡選出一個或是一些你認為合適的答案）

(1)讓西方哲學家注意到自然現象的本質。

(2)讓西方哲學家注意到現象的相互關係。

(3)讓歐洲的哲學接近科學。

(4)讓西方的哲學進一步接近中國的哲學。

(5)上面四個答案都不合適（請你必定簡單的寫出你的意見）。

A. Counterfactual Stories: Version Three (cont.)

Bier was an 18th century European philosopher who wanted very much to investigate the principles of the universe and the laws of nature. Because there was some contact between China and Europe at that time, Chinese philosophical works could be found in Europe; but none had been translated. Bier could not read Chinese, but if he had been able to read Chinese he would have found that while Western philosophers generally investigated natural phenomena as individual entities, Chinese philosophers generally investigated natural phenomena in terms of their mutual interrelationships. If Bier had read Chinese philosophy he would certainly have been influenced by it, have synthesized it with Western philosophy, and have created a theory which not only explained natural phenomena as individual entities, but which also made clear their interrelationships. This theory would not only have overcome a weakness in the Western philosophy of that time, but also would have had a deep influence on German, French, and Dutch philosophy leading them closer to science.

Please indicate, by choosing *one or more* of the following answers, what contribution or contributions Bier made to the West according to the paragraph above:

1.   Bier led Western philosophy to pay attention to natural phenomena as individual entities.
2.   He led Western philosophy to pay attention to the mutual interrelationships among natural phenomena.
3.   He led European philosophy closer to science.
4.   He led Western philosophy one step closer to Chinese philosophy.
5.   None of these answers are appropriate. (Please explain your own opinion briefly)

B. Triangle-to-circle question (See text for English version)

假如所有的圈圈都很大，如果這個小三角形"△"是一個圓圈，那麼這個三角形是不是很大？

C. Sentence Transformations (see text for English Version)

請你先看下面的兩個例子，然後再按照例句的情形把下面的三句話寫出來：

例：艾豪跟玲慧結婚了→艾豪跟玲慧的婚姻。

這件事情很重要→這件事情的重要性。

(1) 可能他已經到了→

(2) 艾豪成功了→

(3) 他對這件事情的態度很誠懇→

D. Polluted Environment Stories: (See text for English version) Version One (Conditional version)

最近有一篇研究空氣污染的報告說：住在空氣污染的地方，會使人得肺癌。但是，住在空氣污染，地勢比較高的地方，更有危險性。反之，住在空氣污染，地勢低的地方，危險性也低。奇怪的是，住在空氣污染，地勢比較高的地方，如果又多吃肥肉，那麼就變成跟住在地勢低的地方一樣了。

按照上文，指出下面哪種情形，對身體最有壞處？

① 住在空氣污染，地勢低的地方，同時又吃很多肥肉。

② 住在空氣污染，地勢高的地方，同時又吃很多肥肉。

③ 住在空氣污染，地勢高的地方，同時少吃肥肉。

④ 問得很糊塗。

D. Polluted Environment Stories—(cont.)
    Version Two (Relationship Version)

最近有一篇研究空氣污染的報告說：住在空氣污染的地方跟得肺癌一定有關係。但是，在地勢比較高的地方，這種關係更爲密切。反之，在地勢低的地方，關係較不密切。奇怪的是，住在地勢比較高的地方，如果又多吃肥肉，那麼空氣污染跟肺癌的關係，就跟在地勢低的地方一樣了。

按照上文，指出下面的哪種情形對身體，最有壞處？

①住在空氣污染，地勢低的地方，同時又吃很多肥肉。

②住在空氣污染，地勢高的地方，同時又吃很多肥肉。

③住在空氣污染，地勢高的地方，同時少吃肥肉。

④問得很糊塗。

D. Polluted Environment Stories—(cont.)
    Version Three (Double unspecified relationship version)

李四有個特性：在濕度比較低的時候，天氣越熱，他吃的魚越少，那麼他就覺得越舒服；但是在濕度很高的時候，原來之間的關係反而顛倒過來了。

按照上文，下面的哪兩種情形使李四最不舒服？

①天氣熱   少吃魚   濕度比較低

②天氣熱   少吃魚   濕度很高

③天氣熱   多吃魚   濕度比較低

④天氣熱   多吃魚   濕度很高

⑤天氣冷   多吃魚   濕度比較低

E. Child Raising Discussion (See text for English version)

訓練孩子遵守道德，各人都用不同的方法，有些人利用孩子怕被處罰的心理；就是在孩子做錯事後一定處罰他，那麼孩子因為怕被處罰，所以也就不敢違反道德，也有的人在孩子做對了事以後，一定獎賞孩子，讓孩子自動的喜歡遵守道德。雖然這兩種方法都可以訓練孩子遵守道德，但是第一個方法可能會在孩子的心理上有不太好的影響，也許會減少孩子們的自信心。

按照上文那兩種方法有什麼相同的地方，在下面的答案裡請選出一個來：

(1)兩種法子都沒有用。

(2)沒有什麼相同的地方，因為一個在心理上有不太好的因素。

(3)兩個都會達到訓練孩子遵守道德的目的。

(4)用第二個方法比較好。

(5)這四個答案都沒有道理。（因為什麼請你寫在下面或反面）

Indexes

Author Index

Subject Index

84223

DATE DUE